DAVID **GROVER** / SEVEN **VINTON**

DIGITAL TECHNOLOGIES FOR THE AUSTRALIAN CURRICULUM

A PROJECT–BASED APPROACH

YEARS 7 AND 8

Digital Technologies for the Australian Curriculum: A Project-based Approach
Years 7 & 8
1st Edition
David Grover
Seven Vinton
Contributors: Heather Knights and Eamon Gormley

Publishing editors: Julie McArthur and Lizzie Allmand
Project editor: Kathryn Coulehan
Proofreader: Bree DeRoche
Cover design: Aisling Gallagher
Text design: Aisling Gallagher
Cover image: iStock.com / Veronaa
Permissions researcher: Helen Mammides
Production controllers: Karen Young and Christine Fotis
Typeset by: MPS Limited

Any URLs contained in this publication were checked for currency during the production process. Note, however, that the publisher cannot vouch for the ongoing currency of URLs.

For product information and technology assistance,
in Australia call **1300 790 853**;
in New Zealand call **0800 449 725**

For permission to use material from this text or product, please email
aust.permissions@cengage.com

Cengage Learning Australia
Level 7, 80 Dorcas Street
South Melbourne, Victoria Australia 3205

Cengage Learning New Zealand
Unit 4B Rosedale Office Park

For learning solutions, visit **cengage.com.au**

Printed in China by 1010 Printing International Limited
12 13 14 15 26 25 24

National Library of Australia Cataloguing-in-Publication Data
Grover, David, author.
Digital Technologies for the Australian Curriculum:
A Project-based Approach Years 7 and 8 /
David Grover ; Seven Vinton.

9780170411813 (paperback)

Information technology--Curriculum planning.
Computer programming--Study and teaching (Secondary)
Information technology--Australia--Textbooks.
Computer software--Problems, exercises, etc.
Software maintenance--Textbooks.

Vinton, Seven, author.

CONTENTS

INTRODUCTION

Digital Technologies for the Australian Curriculum: A Project-based Approach is a project-based creative resource for students and teachers, comprehensively covering all Stage 4 and 5 outcomes for the Australian Curriculum: Digital Technologies.

The two workbooks, one for each stage, together with accompanying online resources, establish students' knowledge in the core Knowledge and Understanding topics, then build understanding using a variety of learning approaches such as guided projects, knowledge probes, skill builders, activities, class group work, web probes and research tasks.

After acquiring a topic's necessary foundational skills, students build practical skills by developing their own digital solutions through a selection of practical projects.

Reflecting the pattern established in the curriculum, all projects follow the progression: Defining, Designing, Implementing and Evaluating.

Teachers can select from over 40 individual and group-based projects in five topic areas serving a wide range of ability levels. The projects emphasise creativity and challenge while building on essential knowledge and skills. Many include further extensions or advanced options. Online teacher resources offer a variety of options for flexible implementation in the school.

Key ideas specified in the digital technologies curriculum of project management, systems thinking, design thinking, computational thinking and creating preferred futures are addressed.

The workbooks and associated online resources embrace the curriculum's core competencies of literacy, numeracy, ICT, critical and creative thinking, personal and social capability, ethical understanding and intercultural understanding.

HOW TO USE THIS BOOK

Digital Technologies for the Australian Curriculum: A Project-based Approach Years 7 and 8 is divided into two parts. Part One: Knowledge and Understanding covers the **core** units outlined by the curriculum and Part Two: Projects provides opportunities for students to explore the concepts and skills discussed earlier and to test their knowledge of digital technology through the application of IT skills. The book has the following features:

- **ACARA outcomes** are listed on chapter opening pages where applicable.
- **Glossary terms** are listed on chapter opening pages where applicable and highlighted in text.
- **Infobits** provide snippets of useful and interesting information to stimulate curiosity.
- **Web probes** encourage students to go online and complete further investigations.
- **Activities** contain a variety of practical tasks that can be completed as a class in groups, individually or as homework.

- **Knowledge probes** highlight activities that require greater depth of discovery and higher-order thinking.
- **Skill builders** are tasks that will develop a particular skill.
- **Data files** such as Excel spreadsheets, coding files and images required by students to complete certain projects or activities can be found on the *Digital Technologies 7 & 8* website: https://www.nelsonnet.com.au/free-resources/nelson-technology/digital-technologies-7-8-workbook-1ed. These resources are freely accessible for students and teachers who have registered for a free NelsonNet account.
- **Weblinks** to useful websites are supplied on the *Digital Technologies 7 & 8* website.
- **Screenshots** are included throughout to provide students with clear visual cues to follow.

9780170411813

ABOUT THE AUTHORS

David Grover has been Head Teacher of Computing at Chatswood High School, New South Wales and is the author of a number of texts and online resources for the Australian Curriculum in Digital Technologies and for senior secondary computing. He conducts workshops in computing technology for teachers at a number of tertiary institutions and has served as a senior examination marker.

David has conducted research in educational applications of augmented reality (AR) and in digital creativity for learning for Macquarie University and at present is enjoying combining AR with 3D printing! He loves sharing his excitement for emerging technologies with students and many have gone on to enjoy successful careers in animation, games design, robotics and programming. He has established a reputation for his expertise in interactive digital education, recognised in various teaching awards and a NSW Premier's Scholarship where he studied New and Emerging Technologies in educational institutions around the globe.

Seven Vinton is the co-inventor of the ARD2-INNOV8 Shield for Arduino. Prior to his 18 years of teaching, Seven worked in the areas of industrial arts and technologies, running a small business in ceramic parts and mold-making. He has enjoyed a life-long passion for digital technologies, and has currently completed programming courses in C++, Python, MATLAB, IoT and Digital Interfacing.

Seven currently holds the position of Curriculum Leader at Oberon High School in Geelong and also teaches classes in VCE Studio Arts, Engineering, and Digital Technologies. He has held several other leadership positions in his teaching career, including VCAL Coordinator, Professional Learning Leader, and eLearning Leader. Seven has run and participated in many regional and state-level presentations that have been aimed at building capacity of digital learning for both students and teachers.

Seven has dedicated much of his time over the past four years towards finding and promoting solutions that help support students with programming digital devices.

UNDERSTANDING DIGITAL SYSTEMS

01

GLOSSARY

central processing unit (CPU) Main chip in a computer, performing data processing and control

digital solution Final version of a digital or information system designed to fulfill a given need

digital system A collection of hardware and software components. A computer is part of a digital system. Digital systems transform data and can be connected to form networks

information system Digital systems combined with data, processes and people to collect, organise and communicate information

input Data put into a digital system for processing via an input device such as a keyboard or sensor

output Data produced by a digital system and typically delivered to an output device such as a printer, monitor or actuator

processing Changing data from one form to another

RAM Random-access memory. Primary volatile (non-permanent) data storage device

ROM Read-only memory. Primary non-volatile (permanent) data storage device

sensor Input device that accepts data from the environment

WHAT IS A COMPUTER?

The very first computer was a person!

From the 1600s up until the mid-twentieth century the word computer referred to a person who carried out calculations or computations.

Around the 1850s with the invention of the first calculating machines, the term computer began to be used for these machines that carried out calculations.

Figure 1.1 An example of an early computing machine.

Computers are the most complex machine ever invented. A computer is an example of a digital system. It is made up of hardware (physical devices) and software (programs).

When supplied with data the computer processes the data and stores or displays results. A computer is really a data **processing** machine.

In *Digital Technologies 9 & 10* we will have a detailed look at how a computer works. Here we look at the 'big picture'.

DIGITAL AND INFORMATION SYSTEMS

What is a digital system?

A **digital system** is a collection of hardware and software components. Digital systems transform data and can be connected to form networks (including the Internet). Digital systems are at the heart of the study of digital technologies.

A computer is just one part of a digital system.

What is an information system?

Information systems are digital systems that have been combined with data, processes and people to collect, organise and communicate information. The data they **output** becomes information when given meaning by people.

Information systems create **digital solutions**. People use information systems to create a digital solution to a problem or task.

You will be creating your own information systems as part of the projects you undertake during this course.

Today, information systems impact all our lives, in both positive and negative ways. In *Digital Technologies 9 & 10* we will examine these impacts in more detail.

A smartphone is now more like a computer than a phone.

A personal computer might be small enough to sit on your lap, yet powerful enough to act as a server on a network.

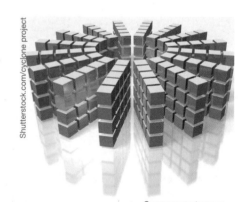
Supercomputers are used for weather forecasting and scientific research.

Network servers are housed in cabinets and are easily removed and replaced.

Mainframe computers are used by banks to process millions of transactions per day.

Figure 1.2 Computers come in lots of different shapes and sizes. They are usually grouped by both size and purpose.

9780170411813

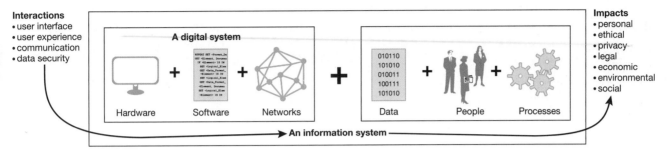

Figure 1.3 An information system is created when a digital system becomes part of a larger system, along with data, people and processes.

HARDWARE COMPONENTS OF A COMPUTER SYSTEM

A computer system is part of a digital system. The hardware components of a computer system get their names from the task each one performs:

- Input
- Output
- Storage
- Processing and control.

Input

An **input** device collects data from the outside world and changes it into a form suitable for the computer. The keyboard, mouse or touchpad are the most common input devices. The computer converts the press of a key into an electrical signal transmitted to the system box. This data is stored in memory until it can be processed by the **central processing unit (CPU)**.

Microphones, scanners, digital cameras and graphics tablets are all common input devices.

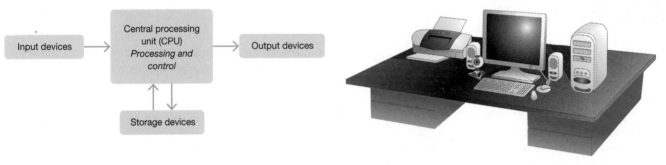

Figure 1.4 Most devices connected to the computer are controlled by the central processing unit. Categorise items shown on the desktop using the four categories identified in the diagram to the left.

Activity: Smartphone sensors

Sensors are input devices used to collect data such as temperature, light, noise, acceleration and movement, which they send to a central processing unit.

Table 1.1 lists some of the sensors used for input to a computer that most of us use every day – the smartphone! A smartphone has more ways to receive data than a desktop computer or laptop! Individually, or as part of a group, copy and complete this table. If in a group, use a collaborative tool such as Google sheets.

Table 1.1

Sensor	What does it measure?	Use (e.g. by an app?)	Does your phone have one? ✓ or X	Explanation of operation
Proximity sensor				
Ambient light sensor				
Front camera				

Sensor	What does it measure?	Use (e.g. by an app?)	Does your phone have one? ✓ or X	Explanation of operation
Rear camera				
Accelerometer				
Gyroscope				
Compass				
Barometer				
Near-field communication (NFC)				
Touch fingerprint scanner				
Temperature				
Other				

Output

An output device communicates data from the computer's central processing unit (CPU) to users. Information may be output as a display on a monitor or printer, or it may be output as sounds from a speaker.

Monitors convert data in the form of digital electrical signals from the system into patterns of light, which are interpreted by our brain as text or images. Most monitors have flat screens and use liquid crystal display (LCD) technology.

Head-up displays, 3D printers and laser cutters can also function as output devices. Speakers take electrical signals output by a computer and convert them into sound waves, perhaps speech, music or sound effects.

How many output components can you list for a typical smartphone?

A fellow student asks you how a computer monitor works. Look at the illustration (Figure 1.5) of the operation of a liquid crystal display (LCD) computer monitor and then read the descriptions of the different parts below. Match the numbers from the illustration (1–6) to the correct description and then reorder these descriptions into the correct sequence.

A A polarising filter only lets through the light waves that are vibrating horizontally. _____

B A second polarising filter only lets through light vibrating in a vertical plane. _____

C One of three coloured filters then colours the light red, green or blue. _____

D Light from a fluorescent panel spreads in waves that vibrate in all directions. _____

E The mixture of colours on the front panel combine. In this example, full red, half green and no blue will result in a pixel appearing pale brown. _____

F The light waves then pass through the liquid crystal layer. Each crystal cell is charged by varying amounts to twist the vibration of the wave. _____

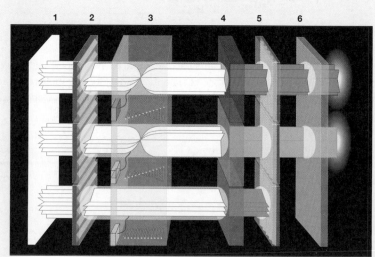

Figure 1.5

Despite predictions that computers would lead to paperless offices, they are still popular output devices. Imagine that your younger brother or sister asks you how a laser printer works.

Referring to this figure, write a paragraph explanation for them.

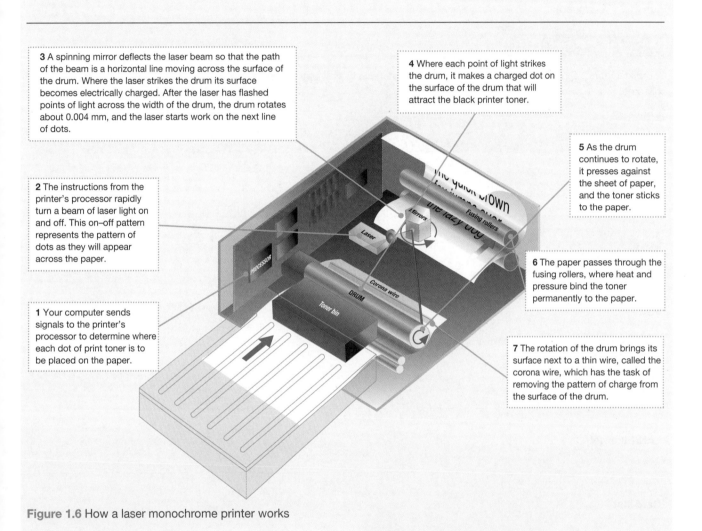

3 A spinning mirror deflects the laser beam so that the path of the beam is a horizontal line moving across the surface of the drum. Where the laser strikes the drum its surface becomes electrically charged. After the laser has flashed points of light across the width of the drum, the drum rotates about 0.004 mm, and the laser starts work on the next line of dots.

4 Where each point of light strikes the drum, it makes a charged dot on the surface of the drum that will attract the black printer toner.

5 As the drum continues to rotate, it presses against the sheet of paper, and the toner sticks to the paper.

2 The instructions from the printer's processor rapidly turn a beam of laser light on and off. This on–off pattern represents the pattern of dots as they will appear across the paper.

6 The paper passes through the fusing rollers, where heat and pressure bind the toner permanently to the paper.

1 Your computer sends signals to the printer's processor to determine where each dot of print toner is to be placed on the paper.

7 The rotation of the drum brings its surface next to a thin wire, called the corona wire, which has the task of removing the pattern of charge from the surface of the drum.

Figure 1.6 How a laser monochrome printer works

Ports for input and output

Input and output devices, such as keyboards, monitors or printers, are often attached by cables to the computer. The port is the interface, or point of attachment, of these devices to the system box. There are different types of ports depending on the device being connected. Common ports on a laptop are USB, HDMI, VGA, LAN, DVI.

Ethernet   DVI   Firewire   USB   Microphone   Headphones

Figure 1.7 This page: Ports on a laptop. Next page: A selection of common USB plugs. Some laptops use only one type of multipurpose port, USBC/Thunderbolt 3.

Figure 1.7 *(Continued)*

Web probe: Ports

Complete Table 1.2 by describing the function of each of these typical laptop ports and give examples of the type of data collected, stored or output from each device.

Table 1.2

Port	What is it used for?
USB	
HDMI	
VGA	
Memory card reader	
LAN/Ethernet	
Card slot	
DVI	
USB-C/Thunderbolt 3	

Storage

A computer needs a way to store the data as you work on it. This is performed automatically by the computer system and is called primary storage. It is the only memory the CPU can access directly.

Primary storage comes in two varieties: **RAM** (random-access memory), which is lost when the power is turned off and **ROM** (read-only memory). You will learn more about these later in this chapter when we discuss the CPU and the motherboard.

The second type of memory is called secondary storage and is sometimes called external memory. Hard disk drives (HDD) and solid state drives (SSD) are both commonly used for secondary storage. Secondary storage saves files and programs permanently, even when the power is turned off. You will already understand the importance of saving files to a hard disk while you are working with them and before you turn your computer off. Average internal SSD hard drives have a capacity of around 500 GB to 1 TB and are fast and reliable but more expensive than an internal HDD, which typically have larger storage capacity than SSD.

We can also store data in the cloud on remote servers. Networked and online file servers are designed to allow secure storage of data and are accessible across the Internet. These are large groups of hard drives located in remote places.

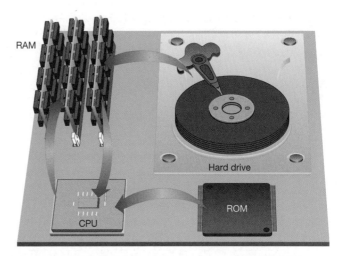

RAM

Hard drive

ROM

CPU

Figure 1.9 When data moves from a chip, such as RAM, ROM or the CPU, to a HDD hard disk, it needs to be changed from a pattern of high and low voltages to a pattern of magnetic regions. Changes in the direction of magnetisation are used to represent binary data bits.

Shutterstock.com/Faraways

Thinkstock/bedo

Series of RAM chips

Thinkstock/Alexey Pereverzev

Thinkstock/Philip Lange

Hard disk drive

Flash memory stick

Figure 1.8 Primary storage (RAM chips) and secondary storage (HDD and memory stick)

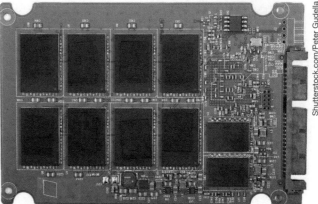

Shutterstock.com/Peter Gudella

Figure 1.10 Top: Inside a hard drive (HDD). Bottom: A solid state drive (SSD). The HDD uses a head that moves across the platter seeking the correct sector for reading data. The SSD has no moving parts and virtually instant access to its data, but is more expensive.

Table 1.3 Three data storage devices. Hard disks are coated with a magnetic material. The read-write head of a disk drive magnetises a spot on the surface to record the data, which can later be read.

Data storage type	Bit represented as	
RAM chip	Voltage high or low in a register	11001010
Magnetic hard disk	Polarity of magnetised particle	11001010
Optical disc	Detection of edges of pits	11001010

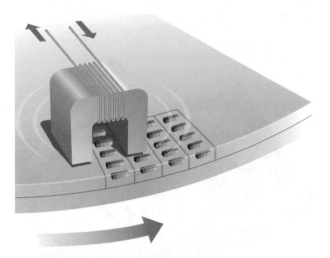

Figure 1.11 Hard disks are coated with a magnetic material. The read-write head of a disk drive magnetises a spot on the surface to record the data, which can later be read back.

Figure 1.12 At a Google Data Centre in Belgium, failed hard drives are being destroyed on site to protect user data.

Web probe: Storage

Research the advantages and disadvantages of various forms of storage and complete Table 1.4.

Table 1.4

Storage method	Advantages	Disadvantages	Typical capacity in GB	When would you use it?
DVD				
Flash (USB) stick				
HDD				
SSD				
The cloud				

1 Table 1.5 helps to understand storage sizes for different types of data. Complete the centre column of this table. Although memory capacity is usually measured in powers of 2, for simplicity use the nearest power of 10.
2 Find out what ZB stands for, and how big it is in bytes.

Knowledge
Probe

Table 1.5

Size	How many bytes?	Typical example
1 bit		Answer to a yes/no question
1 byte	1 byte	A single letter of the alphabet
90 bytes	90 bytes	A line of text from a book
0.5 KB		Typical sector of a hard disk
4 KB		One page of text from a novel
1 MB		1024×1024 pixel bitmap image using 256 colours
3 MB		A three-minute song
650–900 MB		A CD-ROM
1 GB		One hour of an SD streamed movie
8 GB		Size of a regular flash drive
4 TB		Size of a $150 hard disk
1.3 ZB		Size of the entire Internet in 2016

INFOBIT

Many laptops now use SSD secondary storage (such as Flash memory) but Google and others are still the biggest buyers of cheaper, although less reliable, HDD hard disk magnetic drives.

Web probe: What is a floppy disk?

The earliest storage for home computers was cassette tape! Following this, floppy disks were used. Find out what these looked like, why they were called floppy disks, and how they stored data. Record your research results on a piece of paper.

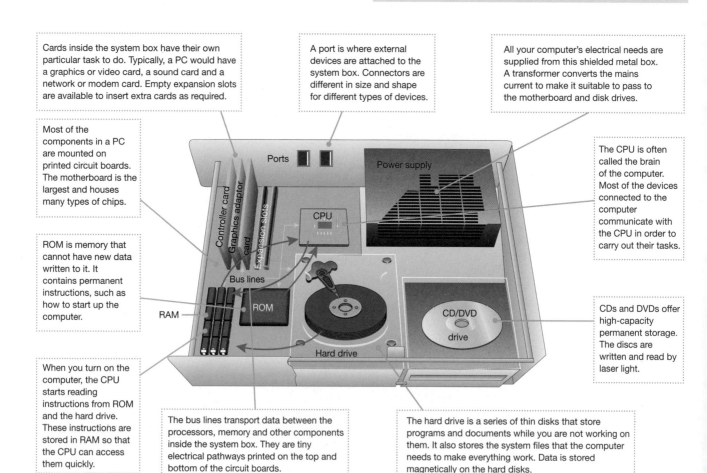

Cards inside the system box have their own particular task to do. Typically, a PC would have a graphics or video card, a sound card and a network or modem card. Empty expansion slots are available to insert extra cards as required.

A port is where external devices are attached to the system box. Connectors are different in size and shape for different types of devices.

All your computer's electrical needs are supplied from this shielded metal box. A transformer converts the mains current to make it suitable to pass to the motherboard and disk drives.

Most of the components in a PC are mounted on printed circuit boards. The motherboard is the largest and houses many types of chips.

The CPU is often called the brain of the computer. Most of the devices connected to the computer communicate with the CPU in order to carry out their tasks.

ROM is memory that cannot have new data written to it. It contains permanent instructions, such as how to start up the computer.

CDs and DVDs offer high-capacity permanent storage. The discs are written and read by laser light.

When you turn on the computer, the CPU starts reading instructions from ROM and the hard drive. These instructions are stored in RAM so that the CPU can access them quickly.

The bus lines transport data between the processors, memory and other components inside the system box. They are tiny electrical pathways printed on the top and bottom of the circuit boards.

The hard drive is a series of thin disks that store programs and documents while you are not working on them. It also stores the system files that the computer needs to make everything work. Data is stored magnetically on the hard disks.

Figure 1.13 Inside a desktop computer's system box

Processing and control

The main item inside the system box is called a motherboard and houses a variety of components, including the all-important chips (see Figure 1.13).

Computer chips are made up of millions of tiny components called transistors, which act as electronic switches. We have already learned that the main chip, the CPU, is responsible for the processing and control of data. It is often referred to as the brain of the computer.

Watch the video 'How a CPU is made'. Do an Internet search of this video title to find it.

Chips come in lots of flavours! The CPU is a microprocessor that works at high speed (more than a billion operations per second!) and needs other chips, like RAM (random-access memory) and ROM (read-only memory) to hold data while it is working.

RAM is volatile, which means it loses its data when power is switched off. That is why you need to save files to secondary storage devices such as a hard disk.

ROM chips hold information that the CPU needs on a regular basis, such as when a computer is starting up. ROM chips hold their content even after power is switched off.

Other chips are designed to perform specific tasks, such as numeric calculations or video decompression. This increases the overall speed of an application as they relieve the CPU of routine tasks.

All these components are connected on the motherboard by bus lines, forming electrical paths between them.

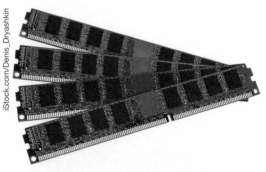

Figure 1.14 An Intel i7 CPU chip

Figure 1.16 Read-only memory (ROM) chips

Figure 1.15 Random-access memory (RAM) chips

Figure 1.17 Old hardware e-waste

Class activity: Hardware dig

Imagine you have dug up evidence of an ancient civilization.

Your teacher will place old hardware around the room and number each item. These may include parts of old or broken computers, or peripherals that are no longer used or new or emerging hardware. Imagine these are evidence of an extinct sophisticated culture that once used computers.

Your group task is to identify each item and decide if its function is input, output, processing, storage or other.

Afterwards your group will be given one item to research in detail and will then present their findings to the class.

Collecting evidence

Use a collaborative tool such as Google Sheets to create a table for your group and identify as many items as possible. Label each: input, output, processing, storage or other.

In-depth research

Your teacher will offer you a choice in a lucky dip of exhibit numbers. This will be the single hardware item that you will research and report on to the class.

You are to cover the following:
- the approximate original price in today's money
- the year of invention
- the inventor
- a brief description of the item
- typical use of the item
- popularity of the item
- the impact on society
- what replaced it or what you think might replace it in future.

SOFTWARE

Software is just a list of instructions that allows data to be processed by the hardware and is created using a range of programming languages. In this course you will learn how to write your own software programs. There are three types of software: operating system software, application software and utility software.

Operating system software

On a personal computer, an operating system controls a computer's hardware. Microsoft® Windows®, Apple's OS and UNIX are the most widely used operating systems around the world.

The operating system is the first thing we see on the screen when we start up a computer. It provides the interface that asks us to log on, or it displays the desktop and its icons. Similarly, when we close down the computer, it tells us that it is logging off and it closes the files in a systematic order before it powers off the hardware.

Embedded systems

Some hardware equipment, such as microwave ovens, dishwashers and other home appliances, or anti-lock braking systems on cars, are designed with an operating system and application software embedded and respond quickly and reliably. They perform as small single purpose computers.

In Chapter 10 you will have the chance to create your own embedded system.

Application software

Most people are familiar with application software such as word processors, image editors like Photoshop and web browsers able to perform a range of tasks in creating, editing, formatting and displaying documents. It is application software that allows computers to perform a wide variety of processing tasks. Increasingly, people are creating their own applications (apps) for mobile devices. These small applications perform a single or limited task and can often be created using open-source (free), user-friendly software.

Utility software

A third type of software, called utility software, has specific tasks to perform, usually 'housekeeping' such as file management, print management or virus protection.

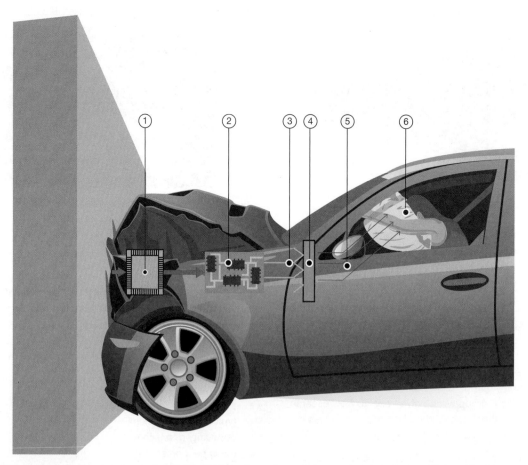

Figure 1.18 The airbag system in a car is an embedded system. An accelerometer detects a collision (1), this signal is processed by the hardware and software of the bag system board (2) and if strong enough sends current to heat an element (3) causing a chemical reaction (4) and explosion that produces nitrogen gas (5) and inflates the bag (6).

Class activity: What makes great software?

Your task is to reach agreement with as many other people as possible on what makes great software, using a decision-making activity.

You will finish off by writing an online review of a piece of software using a blog.

Stage 1

On your own, write down three features you feel make excellent software (example: the icons are easy to understand). It may help to look at the software titles in the list above Table 1.8 on the next page. Record your chosen features in Table 1.7, Stage 1.

Stage 2

You have five minutes to move from person to person to find someone who will agree with the three features you chose in Stage 1. Either of you may adjust what you wrote in order to reach complete agreement on the three features. If you can't find a partner, stand by yourself with your original three features.

If you are successful, sit down in a pair and record the three features in Table 1.7, Stage 2.

Stage 3

Your pair now tries to find another pair to form a group of four.

You have five minutes to find another group or person in the room who will agree with your group, or who is willing to alter their list so all agree on the same three features.

Your group sits down together and records three features in Table 1.7, Stage 3.

Stage 4

Repeat until all class has met every other group and no more agreement is possible between groups.

Table 1.7

Stage 1	Stage 2
Stage 3	**Stage 4**

Class discussion

Your teacher will lead a discussion by asking a spokesperson from each of the final groups to read the three features they came up with. Have someone record these for the class.

Guided by your teacher, the whole class must now agree on a final class list of no more than five features of great software. Write these in the space below.

_____

_____

_____

_____

_____

Software evaluation

On your own or with a partner, compare two items of software with similar purposes using the evaluation criteria developed by your class.

You may choose to compare an online versus a standalone version of the same software (e.g. Photoshop).

Your teacher may choose to allow you a choice or may issue the same two applications to all the class and have the class compare responses. Try to avoid being biased towards applications with which you are most familiar.

Suggested software applications to compare:

- Windows versus MacOS
- Firefox versus Chrome
- Photoshop versus GIMP (free)
- Microsoft Word versus Google Docs
- Dropbox versus Google Drive
- Powerpoint versus Google Slides or Keynote
- Excel versus Google Sheets
- Weebly versus Wix

Note: Score the software out of five for each of your criteria.

Table 1.8

Software title	What it does	Criterion 1	Criterion 2	Criterion 3	Criterion 4	Criterion 5	Comments

Blog review

On your own, create an online blog using a site such as WordPress or Blogger and write a brief review comparing two similar software titles.

REVIEW

Identify

1 What are the four main parts of a computer system?

_____

_____

2 What is a digital system?

_____

_____

_____

3 What is an information system?

_____

_____

_____

4 What is the difference between data and information?

_____

_____

_____

_____

Analyse

5 Compare a HDD with a SSD as a secondary storage device.

_____

_____

_____

_____

6 Outline the differences between RAM and ROM.

_____

_____

_____

_____

7 Arrange these prefixes in order of increasing size: giga, peta, kilo, mega, tera.

_____

8 How is an embedded system different to a standard computer operating system?

_____

_____

_____

_____

_____

Investigate

9 List the hardware devices and their details installed as part of your computer system.

_____

_____

_____

_____

_____

_____

02

UNDERSTANDING DATA

GLOSSARY

analog data Data represented by values, which vary continuously, e.g. time, live music, traditional photographs

ASCII A numeric code used to represent 128 specific characters in computer systems, including 0–9, A–Z and a–z

binary A base 2 number system typically using the two symbols 0 and 1 to represent switches as being either off or on. This system is particularly suited to digital computers contain switches in the form of integrated circuits comprising many transistor switches

bit A binary digit. The smallest digital data item a computer can process. A binary digit can have only two values, most often represented by either a 0 or 1

bit depth Number of bits available to represent a pixel's colour (also known as colour depth)

bitmap The result of mapping items to bits (binary digits 0 and 1) and most often referring to graphics or images (but can be other forms of media). Bitmapped images (also known as paint or raster images) are ones in which each 'dot', or pixel, is represented by a number mapped to its colour

byte Package of 8 bits

data Information in its unorganised or raw form; the representation of information using numerical codes

data type Category of data defining its possible values and its method of storage and processing by a computer, e.g. text, graphics, audio

digital data Data represented by fixed values rather than a continuous spectrum of values, e.g. integers, alphabets

file format Particular structure used to store various data files, e.g. jpeg, tif, gif are different file formats for storing bitmap images

Hertz (Hz) Standard unit of measurement for frequency equal to one cycle per second

information Data that has been given meaning by people; data given context and organisation

sample rate Describes the number of samples taken each second when digitising analog data

Unicode A method for digital encoding text from most of the world's writing systems. Includes ASCII as a subset

vector Images represented by geometric descriptions such as points, lines, curves and shapes. Vector images are also known as draw images

WAYS WE REPRESENT OUR WORLD

Figure 2.2 Computers represent and process many different kinds of data using only 0s and 1s.

Knowledge probe: Warm-up discussion

As a class discussion, or on your own, consider:

1 How would you communicate with
- a person from another culture and no shared language?
- a being from another planet?
2 In which ways is a computer different from a human brain?

Knowledge Probe

INTRODUCTION

From the earliest times human beings have invented ways to represent the world around them. We have done this by using words, numbers, art and symbols (see Figure 2.1).

Around the middle of last century, computers became another tool we could use. But computers have an advantage, because they do more than just represent **data** – they can process it! We rely on computing technology to reliably process huge amounts and kinds of data such as text, numbers, images, audio, video, animation and computer code.

In this chapter you will be discovering how computers represent and process so many different kinds of data using only **binary** code – just 0s and 1s.

DATA VERSUS INFORMATION

People often confuse the terms 'data' and 'information'. Imagine a list of numbers on a piece of paper. In this form, it is just data. However, if someone told you that the numbers were telephone numbers, then they would have some meaning. It is human understanding that changes data into information.

Data can be letters or numbers, patterns of dots, or electrical or light signals but it only becomes information when it is given meaning by people.

Figure 2.1 Information has been recorded and displayed in many forms over thousands of years, from early cave paintings to signs drawn on the ground, cuneiform, hieroglyphics and scrolls. Johannes Gutenberg printed his first book (a Bible) in 1455. The idea of a book has now evolved into electronic displays such as e-readers.

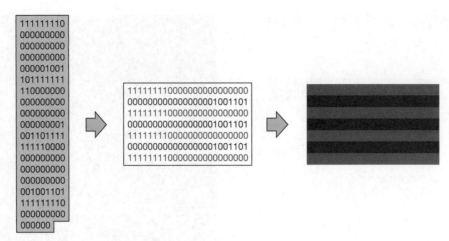

Figure 2.3 Raw data becomes information when given meaning by people. Here raw data in binary form is interpreted by a computer as seven sets of codes. A human being may then interpret this as the background pattern of a flag. Other interpretations are possible too.

CAPTURING AN ANALOG WORLD USING BINARY CODE

Most of the **information** we receive from the world around us comes in quantities that vary continuously. For example, the changing frequencies making the music we hear, or the graduations of colour in an image, like in Figure 2.4. If values vary smoothly like this, we refer to them as **analog data**. These are impossible to represent using **digital data**, which describe only 'fixed jumps' in values.

Figure 2.4 This painting in its original form shows continuous graduations of paint, but when the image is digitised these can only be approximated by fixed digital values.

In the past engineers used analog slide rules (see Figure 2.5) as computing devices. Modern computers are digital and need to convert or digitise analog data to process it.

Figure 2.5 Slide rules are analog calculators.

Complete Table 2.1 by identifying a suitable method for digitising these real world analog **data types** for processing by a computer.

Table 2.1

Analog data type	Method of capture (digitalising)
Text	
Image	
Audio	*Recording using a microphone*
Animation	
Video	

Once we have the digitised data, how does a computer process it?

Digital computers are built using switches that are either 'on' or 'off' and work very fast and accurately. Originally, computer switches were mechanical (see Figure 2.7, opposite page), the next generation used vacuum tubes, the next used transistors and today computers use integrated circuits (see Figure 2.8, opposite page) each containing billions of transistors acting as switches.

9780170411813

Figure 2.7 The Altair was one of the first home computers and used switches for input and lights for output.

Figure 2.8 Integrated circuits come in various shapes and sizes.

Modern computers use low voltages or high voltages to represent a 0 or 1. We call these values **binary digits**, or **bits** for short. Real-world analog quantities need to be approximated using just these two symbols. Before we learn how this is done we need to make sure we understand the binary number system.

Web probe: Moore's law

Find out what Moore's law is and explain it by sketching a simple infographic below.

UNDERSTANDING THE BINARY SYSTEM

At first it seems quite difficult to work with binary numbers, but with a little practice it can be fun. You may have already learnt how binary numbers work. Because it is so important in digital technologies, we will revise it here.

Many people think digital means only binary (base 2). This is not true. When we count using the 10 symbols 0–9 we are still counting digitally, although using base 10. It is possible to count in any base. Other important ones are octal (using eight symbols) and hexadecimal (16 symbols).

Counting in base 10 uses all nine symbols in the units column (not counting 0) until they run out. Then we shift 1 into the tens column and start again, and so on. If we use three columns the number of different numbers we can create is 1000 (i.e. 000–999).

To count in binary (also called base 2) we follow exactly the same idea, but we use only two symbols. We could use any symbols, but traditionally we pick 0 and 1, which is appropriate because it reminds us of switches being on or off. Counting in base 2 works the same way as counting in base 10.

Using two columns we can write four different numbers: 00, 01, 10, 11.

Activity: Counting in binary

Column values in the decimal system are powers of 10. In the same way, column values in the binary system columns are powers of 2.

1 Complete the decimal table (Table 2.2) for 1–15 by counting in 1s down the rows using the digits 0–9.
2 Complete the binary table (Table 2.3) for 1–15 by counting in 1s down the rows using only 0 or 1.

   Important: In either table you can find a number's value by adding the column values in the headings. So in binary:
   1 0 1 means $1 \times 4 + 0 \times 2 + 1 \times 1$ (see Table 2.3).

Table 2.2 Decimal

Place value of column	10^2	10^1	10^0	
	100	10	1	
			0	
			1	
			2	
			3	
			4	
			5	
		1	5	$= 1 \times 10 + 5 \times 1$

Table 2.3 Binary

Place value of column	2^7	2^6	2^5	2^4	2^3	2^2	2^1	2^0	
	128	64	32	16	8	4	2	1	
								0	
								1	
							1	0	
							1	1	
						1	0	0	
						1	0	1	$= 1 \times 4 + 0 \times 2 + 1 \times 1$

Class activity: Binary body race

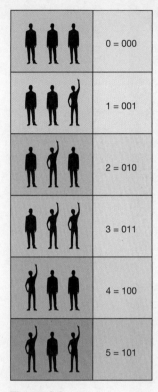

Figure 2.9

Seven students stand in line and count using their raised left hand to represent a '1'.

The example in Figure 2.9 uses three students to illustrate how to count to five. Read the text and study the image to help you understand how to complete this activity.

- Say '1': Right most student (Student 1) raises left hand. We see 1 in binary.
- Say '2': Student 1 cannot count higher, so they drop their hand and tap the shoulder of the next student using right (non-counting) hand. Student 2 raises their left hand.
- Say '3': Student 1 raises left hand again. Student 2 already has left hand up. We see binary 11.
- Say '4': Student 1 cannot count higher, so they drop their left hand and tap the shoulder of Student 2 using right (non-counting) hand. Student 2 cannot count higher, so they drop their left hand and tap Student 3 who then raises their left hand. We see binary 100.
- Say '5': Student 1 raises left hand. Student 3 has hand up already. We see binary 101.

- Keep this pattern going. Try calling the next numbers faster until a mistake is made. Those who make the mistake drop out and are replaced.

Once you understand how the game works you can race two teams to see who can get to 1111111 first.

Figure 2.10

1 a What binary and decimal value is represented in Figure 2.10?

b Circle the row in your binary table (Table 2.3) that represents the number illustrated.

Figure 2.11

2 a What binary and decimal value is represented in Figure 2.11?

b Circle the row in your binary table (Table 2.3) that represents the illustrated number.

3 Write your age in binary.

4 Count to 50 in binary using columns drawn on your own sheet of paper or use a spreadsheet.

This activity is a great way to experience the power of binary.

Copy and cut out these cards.

1	11	21	31	41	51
3	13	23	33	43	53
5	15	25	35	45	55
7	17	27	37	47	57
9	19	29	39	49	59

2	11	22	31	42	51
3	14	23	34	43	54
6	15	26	35	46	55
7	18	27	38	47	58
10	19	30	39	50	59

4	13	22	31	44	53
5	14	23	36	45	54
6	15	28	37	46	55
7	20	29	38	47	60
12	21	30	39	52	

8	13	26	31	44	57
9	14	27	40	45	58
10	15	28	41	46	59
11	24	29	42	47	60
12	25	30	43	56	

16	21	26	31	52	57
17	22	27	48	53	58
18	23	28	49	54	59
19	24	29	50	55	60
20	25	30	51	56	

32	37	42	47	52	57
33	38	43	48	53	58
34	39	44	49	54	59
35	40	45	50	55	60
36	41	46	51	56	

What happens: ask a partner to guess a secret number between 1 and 60. Spread out the cards. The partner points to cards on which their number appears. You immediately guess their number!

The method: sum all first numbers on cards they point to.

This trick works because of the binary system. Can you explain how?

(Clue: Something is special about the numbers on each card)

9780170411813

REVIEW: BINARY AND DECIMAL CONVERSION

Identify

1 Why do computers work with binary bits instead of using decimals?

_____

_____

_____

2 Convert these binary numbers to decimal.
    a 0000 0110   **b** 0110 0011   **c** 1010 1100

_____

3 Convert these decimal numbers to binary.
    a 4   **b** 64   **c** 63

_____

Analyse

4 Write the decimal equivalent of the largest binary number that can be written using 4 bits (1 nibble).

_____

5 Write the decimal equivalent of the largest binary number that can be written using 8 bits (1 byte).

_____

Investigate

6 Search for a good 'decimal to binary conversion tool' on the Internet and use it to check your answers and then use it to convert your postcode to binary. Discuss the obstacles in the way of using binary in daily life.

BINARY DATA TYPES

The only types of data used by early computers were text and numbers. One reason for this was that no one had invented a way to display or print anything else – certainly not images on a screen! Monitors were just white or light-green characters appearing on a black background (see Figure 2.12).

Basic or primitive data types are built into most general-purpose computer languages. They are:

- character (character, char) called text or strings when there is a sequence of them
- integer numbers
- floating-point numbers
- fixed-point numbers
- Boolean: logical values that can be only true or false.

Today computers must also handle audio, images, video and animation, which are types of data common in multimedia (see Figure 2.13, next page).

How do they do this? Computers use a sequence of binary digits, or bits, to represent all data. A sequence such as 01001101 can mean different things at different times to a computer.

If it's going to a speaker it might be a sound. If it's going to a monitor, it might be the colour of a pixel, or it might be part of actual program code.

For example, if 01001101 were a character it would represent the capital letter M, if it were a colour expressed in RGB it would be a very dark blue and if it were an integer it would be 77 (see Figure 2.14, next page).

Getty Images/Future Publishing

Figure 2.12 Early computer monitors were just terminals and monitors showing only white or light-green characters (letters and digits).

Computers need to know what type the binary data is in order to process it.

In the following pages we will study how computers represent text, images, audio, video and animation. In *Digital Technologies 9 & 10* we study the number data types.

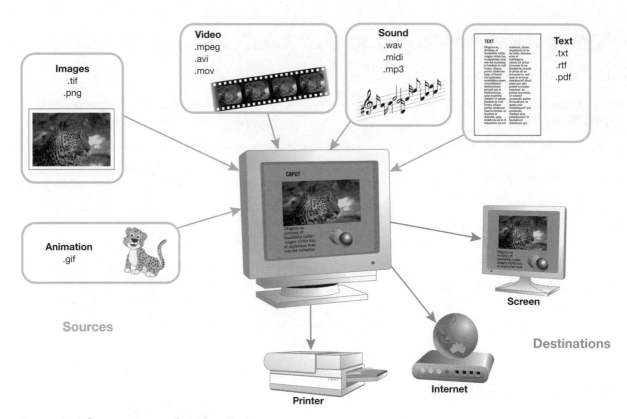

Figure 2.13 Common types of multimedia data

One pattern, many meanings

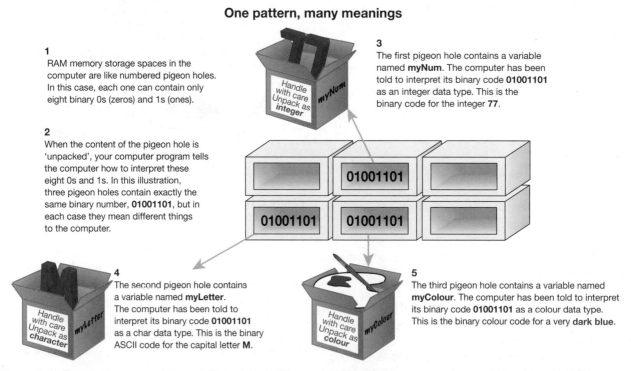

1
RAM memory storage spaces in the computer are like numbered pigeon holes. In this case, each one can contain only eight binary 0s (zeros) and 1s (ones).

2
When the content of the pigeon hole is 'unpacked', your computer program tells the computer how to interpret these eight 0s and 1s. In this illustration, three pigeon holes contain exactly the same binary number, **01001101**, but in each case they mean different things to the computer.

3
The first pigeon hole contains a variable named **myNum**. The computer has been told to interpret its binary code **01001101** as an integer data type. This is the binary code for the integer **77**.

4
The second pigeon hole contains a variable named **myLetter**. The computer has been told to interpret its binary code **01001101** as a char data type. This is the binary ASCII code for the capital letter **M**.

5
The third pigeon hole contains a variable named **myColour**. The computer has been told to interpret its binary code **01001101** as a colour data type. This is the binary colour code for a very **dark blue**.

Figure 2.14 Exactly the same pattern of 0s and 1s, in this case 01001101, can represent very different types of data. Here it can mean either the integer 77, the colour dark blue (in some systems) or the letter M. The computer program needs other information to tell it how it should interpret this binary code. This is known as *declaring* a variable.

REPRESENTING TEXT USING BINARY

A common method to represent text data is called **ASCII** (pronounced 'as-kee') and was published in 1963. The letters stand for American Standard Code for Information Interchange.

ASCII uses 7 bits, allowing 128 different possible codes, with the eighth one sometimes used as a check bit to see if the message was received correctly.

This decision was based on early teleprinters, where paper tape could fit only eight holes across. Holes represented a one. Eight bits can represent 28 = 256 different symbols. Everyone at the time thought that this would be more than enough, as in English there are only 26 letters of the alphabet, upper and lower cases, numerals 0–9, punctuation and some other special symbols.

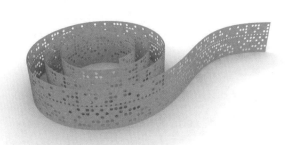

Figure 2.15 Early teleprinter tape could fit only eight holes across each row. The eighth bit was filled with a 0 when it was not used as a check digit.

When we type words in at the keyboard, the signals travel from the keys to the CPU. At this stage of the journey the binary codes are called keyboard scan codes. The computer, however, receives these scan codes and translates them into ASCII to represent the character.

Upper case and lower case to describe capital and small letters of our alphabet got their names from the wooden trays the early typesetters used for storing the individual metal letters they used for composing the lines of text for the early printing presses.

Figure 2.16 Early typesetters separated their metal letters for printing in upper and lower 'cases'.

Here is a small snippet of binary ASCII code:

01000010	01001001	01001110
01000001	01010010	01011001

This is difficult to read, which is why ASCII tables are often written in decimal form. The binary above in decimal looks like this:

66 73 78 65 82 89

See if you can translate this code into a word using the ASCII table in Table 2.4.

Table 2.4 Part of the ASCII table

ASCII decimal	Character	ASCII decimal	Character	ASCII decimal	Character	ASCII decimal	Character
64	@	80	P	96	'	112	p
65	A	81	Q	97	a	113	q
66	B	82	R	98	b	114	r
67	C	83	S	99	c	115	s
68	D	84	T	100	d	116	t
69	E	85	U	101	e	117	u
70	F	86	V	102	f	118	v
71	G	87	W	103	g	119	w
72	H	88	X	104	h	120	x
73	I	89	Y	105	i	121	y
74	J	90	Z	106	j	122	z
75	K	91	[	107	k	123	{
76	L	92	\	108	l	124		
77	M	93	]	109	m	125	}
78	N	94	^	110	n	126	~
79	O	95	_	111	o	127	Delete

Activity: Building an ASCII translator

In this activity we will use a spreadsheet to create a translator for binary ASCII code. We have formed the beginning of a well-known joke about binary. Your task is to discover the rest of the joke and explain it!

You will need to use Fill down and Look up tables, which your teacher will explain. It may be helpful to complete the guided project covering basic spreadsheet skills in Chapter 11 before starting this activity.

You will use your translator to decipher the following message (Table 2.5) written in binary ASCII code (see Figure 2.17). Each byte is a collection of 8 bits arranged as 2 nibbles, making them easier to read.

We have also provided this online as a text file on the *Digital Technologies 7 & 8* website.

Weblink

Table 2.5

01010100	01001000	01000101	01010010	01000101	00100000	01000001	01010010
01000101	00100000	00110001	00110000	00100000	01010100	01011001	01010000
01000101	01010011	00100000	01001111	01000110	00100000	01010000	01000101
01001111	01010000	01001100	01000101	00100000	01001001	01001110	00100000
01010100	01001000	01000101	00100000	01010111	01001111	01010010	01001100
01000100							

1   Create a new spreadsheet with six columns. Add headings to the first row of columns A to F, as shown below. Format the columns using similar colours to those shown here in Table 2.6.

Table 2.6

A	B	C	D	E	F
Message characters as 8 bits	Lookup formula for binary value	Lookup formula for ASCII character		ASCII decimal	ASCII character

2   Enter ASCII decimal codes for the alphabet A–Z, numerals 0–9 and the space character in columns E and F as shown in Table 2.7. Enter the space character for 32. Columns E and F will be used by this spreadsheet to look up the ASCII values.

Table 2.7

	A	B	C	D	E	F
	Message characters as 8 bits	Lookup formula for binary value	Lookup formula for ASCII character		ASCII decimal	ASCII character
1						
2	01010100	=BIN2DEC(A2)	=VLOOKUP(B2,$E$2:$F$38,2)		32	
3	01001000	=BIN2DEC(A3)	=VLOOKUP(B3,$E$2:$F$38,2)		48	0
4	01000101	=BIN2DEC(A4)	=VLOOKUP(B4,$E$2:$F$38,2)		49	1
5	01010010	=BIN2DEC(A5)	=VLOOKUP(B5,$E$2:$F$38,2)		50	2
6	01000101	=BIN2DEC(A6)	=VLOOKUP(B6,$E$2:$F$38,2)		51	3
7	00100000	=BIN2DEC(A7)	=VLOOKUP(B7,$E$2:$F$38,2)		52	4
8	01000001	=BIN2DEC(A8)	=VLOOKUP(B8,$E$2:$F$38,2)		53	5
9	01010010	=BIN2DEC(A9)	=VLOOKUP(B9,$E$2:$F$38,2)		54	6
10	01000101	=BIN2DEC(A10)	=VLOOKUP(B10,$E$2:$F$38,2)		55	7
11	00100000	=BIN2DEC(A11)	=VLOOKUP(B11,$E$2:$F$38,2)		56	8
12	00110001	=BIN2DEC(A12)	=VLOOKUP(B12,$E$2:$F$38,2)		57	9
13	00110000	=BIN2DEC(A13)	=VLOOKUP(B13,$E$2:$F$38,2)		65	A
14	00100000	=BIN2DEC(A14)	=VLOOKUP(B14,$E$2:$F$38,2)		66	B
15	01010100	=BIN2DEC(A15)	=VLOOKUP(B15,$E$2:$F$38,2)		67	C

Figure 2.17

	D	ASCII decimal	ASCII character
1			
2		32	
3		48	0
4		49	1
5		50	2
6		51	3
7		52	4
8		53	5
9		54	6
10		55	7
11		56	8
12		57	9
13		65	A
14		66	B
15		67	C
16		68	D
17		69	E
18		70	F
19		71	G
20		72	H
21		73	I
22		74	J
23		75	K
24		76	L
25		77	M
26		78	N
27		79	O
28		80	P
29		81	Q
30		82	R
31		83	S
32		84	T
33		85	U
34		86	V
35		87	W
36		88	X
37		89	Y
38		90	Z

3 Into cell B2 copy the built-in formula your spreadsheet uses for binary to decimal translation. In Excel and Google Sheets it is:
= BIN2DEC(A2)
Here A2 refers to the cell that contains the binary code. Fill down this formula and check against Figure 2.17.

4 Into cell C2 copy the built-in formula your spreadsheet uses for lookup tables:
= VLOOKUP(B2,$E$2:$F$38,2)
Explanation: VLOOKUP takes the value in cell B2 and looks at the cells of your spreadsheet from E2 to E38 (see Figure 2.17). It returns the value it sees immediately to the right in column F. The '2' means look up the second column of the lookup table. Fill down this formula and check against Figure 2.17.

5 Nearly finished! Finally type 01010100 into cell A2. Translation will occur automatically. The decimal value will appear in cell B2 and the letter 'T' should appear in cell C2.

6 Continue to enter all the binary code in the message down column A. You should finish up at row 42. The complete message will be translated into alphabetic letters down column C.

7 Use the translation to find this complete joke online and see if you can explain it.

What about other languages?

By using 8 bits ASCII can represent 256 different symbols. But computers are not only expected to handle the 26 upper case and 26 lower case Roman or Latin characters used in English. There are many alphabets in use throughout the world.

What about the Russian or Arabic alphabets and how do we represent the many Chinese characters?

To solve this problem another system called **Unicode** was invented. To make it easy to switch, ASCII was included as part of Unicode. Thus, the decimal value of 84 represents upper case 'T' in both systems.

Unicode allows as many as 1 114 112 possible characters. At present, only about 10% of these have been used.

Table 2.8 Unicode solved the problem of representing characters from languages other than English.

Languages	Characters		Unicode	
Greek	Σ	Ω	03A3	03A9
Arabic	ص	ب	0635	0628
Hebrew	ה	ך	05D4	05DA
Cyrillic	Л	Я	041B	042F

Web probe: Unicode

1   Use an online Unicode table to search for a particular language and click on symbols to see their details and Unicode.

2   Which symbols have Unicodes 00E9 and 00FC?

3   Find the Unicode for this Chinese character:

好

What does it mean?

4   Find the Unicodes for these three symbols in Braille:

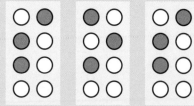

Figure 2.19

Figure 2.18
Unicode logo

 Unicode and the Unicode Logo are registered trademarks of Unicode, Inc. in the United States and other countries

INFOBIT: KLINGON

Klingon is an invented language created for the TV series *Star Trek*. In 1997 someone tried to have the Klingon alphabet registered in Unicode, but this was rejected.

REPRESENTING IMAGES USING BINARY

There are two main methods or formats computers use to represent images. The first is known as **bitmap**, paint or raster. Each pixel ('picture element') has its colour represented in binary code and an image is built up using these.

A popular example of paint software is Adobe's Photoshop (see Figure 2.20). When bitmap images are enlarged they can appear blocky, as each pixel is drawn larger (see Figure 2.21).

Copyright Adobe Photoshop

Figure 2.20 Adobe Photoshop is the best known application for editing bit mapped images.

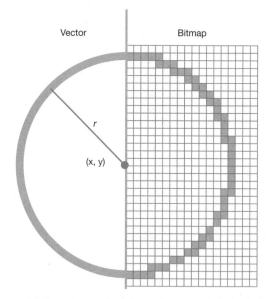

Figure 2.21 A vector and a bitmap image, each depicting part of a circle. The vector image uses a mathematical equation and the bitmap image instead represents the circle's circumference using pixels.

9780170411813

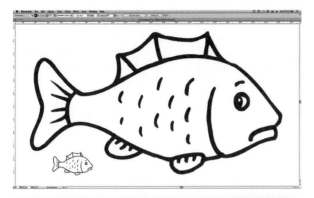

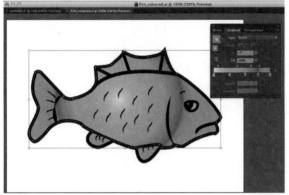

Figure 2.22 Illustrator is a popular application for working with vector images. Top: This fish was copied and enlarged using Adobe Illustrator from a much smaller one, showing how a vector image retains its quality. Bottom: The fish is coloured using both radial and linear gradient fills.

The second is known as **vector** or draw. Images are represented using geometric descriptions with basic built-in shapes (such as a line or a circle), which describe the parts of the image along with information about stroke (line) thickness, colour, texture and fill (see Figure 2.21).

A popular example of vector software is Adobe's Illustrator (see Figure 2.22). Vector-type graphics can be enlarged many times without any loss of quality. The built-in ready-made shapes are simply graphed at a greater size and remain sharp.

Artistry or architecture?

The freeform nature of bitmap applications suits artists, who use distortion, cloning, special filters and many other techniques to modify bitmap images. Paint or bitmap applications exist that imitate actual paint brushes – with pressure sensitivity and paint running out.

On the other hand, the geometric nature of vector applications best suits architects, graphic designers and illustrators, where individual elements of images can be easily reshaped or deleted.

Class activity: Mystery image race

In this activity you will invent a communication protocol in order to convey a simple image to a partner. A protocol is a set of rules for doing something. The first student to recognise what their image is wins.

It is likely the class will invent two methods just like those used in computing.

1 Class divides into two. Pair off with another student from the opposing half of the class. Sit down together and establish a protocol for communicating an image to each other by plotting the image on a sheet of grid paper. At no time are you allowed to let your partner see your sheet of images.

You may choose hand signals or call out coordinates of squares on the grid or shapes, but you are not allowed to describe any image.

Note: The image does not have to be drawn perfectly. The winner only has to say 'yes' when they know what their image is.

2 Partners separate across the room and must not talk.

3 Choose one of the simple drawings provided in Figure 2.23.

Sketch your image on the 10 by 10 grid on the next page. Do not allow your partner to see.

Figure 2.23

From left to right: Shutterstock.com/matius, Shutterstock.com/AVIcon, iStock.com/-VICTOR-, Shutterstock.com/IconBunny, iStock.com/Nik01ay, Shutterstock.com/newelle.

4 Your teacher will signal when to commence.
On the signal, start using your protocol to get your partner to reproduce the same image. Your partner will indicate when they know what the figure is by calling out 'yes' and then confirming it with the teacher.

5 Swap roles and repeat with other partner doing the calling out.

6 Share techniques the class used.

_____

_____

7 Did some images suit one method better than another?

_____

8 Which protocols were best for speed and which were best for accuracy?

_____

_____

9 This activity illustrates differences between bitmap and vector protocols. Can you describe differences between these protocols?

_____

_____

10 Can you suggest which format would occupy the least memory in a computer and explain your answer?

_____

_____

Image bit depth

Let us suppose a child has painted the following image on paper in watercolour (Figure 2.24). Notice that there are gradients in the image. We have learned that computers only understand binary. If this graphic were stored or displayed using only 1 bit per pixel, it could only be represented using two solid colours, or perhaps black and white (1 for black and 0 for white). If we were to use 2 bits per pixel, we could represent four 'colours' (typically greyscale colours). We are faced with this problem: how can our digital computer convert this image to binary code, using only 4 binary digits (i.e. 4 bits) for example? With 4 bits there are only 16 different codes available.

Figure 2.24 Original watercolour painting

To do this exactly is impossible. However, by replacing similar shades of a colour with one colour we can reduce the number of codes needed and still retain a recognisable image. (Figure 2.25). We lay a grid over the top so we have a way to describe the position of each square of colour. In computing these squares are called pixels. Pixel comes from the two words '**pic**ture **el**ement' or the smallest part of an image.

Here we need nine different codes.

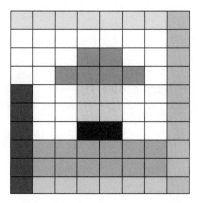

Colour codes
1001
0010
1111
1100
0011
1011
0000
1110
0110

Figure 2.25 Replacing similar shades with single colours

The first three rows of our image can now be described using these three lines of binary numbers:

1001 1001 1001 1001 1001 1001 1001 0010
1111 1111 1111 1111 1111 1111 1111 0010
1111 1111 1111 1100 1100 1111 1111 0010

The amount of colour information in a picture depends upon the number of bits available to represent each pixel's colour and is usually referred to as the colour depth or bit depth.

The greater the number of bits per pixel (i.e. greater bit depth) the more colours that can be represented. The example above used four bits for each colour. Its colour depth is 4 bits per pixel giving 16 possible codes or colours.

More colours means larger files, but higher resolution and clearer images.

Four bits per pixel (16 colours) is suitable for cartoon art.

Eight bits per pixel (256 colours) is used in clipart and low-resolution images.

Twenty-four bits per pixel (16 million colours) gives our eyes the impression of continuous tone, as in a photograph.

INFOBIT

Roses are 1111 1111 0000 0000 0000 0000
Violets are 0000 0000 0000 0000 1111 1111
Just don't forget,
Grass is 0000 0000 1111 1111 0000 0000, too!

Activity: Colouring by numbers

1   Go online and watch the code.org video *Intro to the B & W Pixelation Widget*.
    Then use the code.org widget to complete the following steps: Weblink
    - Create a small image: Start by trying to recreate a 3 × 5 letter 'A' using the pixelation widget.
    - Make your own image of any size of anything you like.
2   First watch the code.org videos *Intro to the Color Pixelation Widget* (*Part 1*, *Part 2*, and (optionally) *Part 3*). Then use the colour pixelation widget at code.org to complete the following:
    - As accurately as you can, reproduce the image in the last activity, approximating the colours as closely as possible.
3   (Advanced) Complete the remaining activities using the widget.

INFOBIT

In 1981, Shigeru Miyamoto drew the famous video game character Mario. Mario wears a cap so his hair does not need to be animated. The moustache avoided the need to draw a mouth and facial expressions on the small onscreen character and so it saves on the number of bits needing to be processed.

Displaying raster and vector images

Even non-bit mapped images such as vector images must be rasterized (i.e. converted to pixels) in order to display them on a computer screen. This is because computer screens are made of pixels and each of these must be switched on or off to produce the correct colour and brightness to display the vector image.

Activity: Bitmap versus vector

1   Use a bitmap-based (paint) software application, such as the tools in Adobe Photoshop or the free image editor GIMP, to create one of the images in the Mystery image race class activity (Figure 2.23).
2   Add colour and texture.
3   Save this file with the name 'yourname_bitmap'.
4   Use a vector-based (draw) software application, such as Adobe Illustrator or Google Drawings to create the same image. Make sure you make this image the same height and width as the bitmap one.
5   Save this file with the name 'yourname_vector'.
6   Inspect the file sizes using your computer. Which task produced the largest file size – bitmap or vector? Why?

Extensions

1   Create your initials using both types of applications.
2   Redesign your house, apartment or backyard using a vector application.

Activity: Comparing bitmap and vector images

1   The following files have been produced for a football tournament.
    • final logo.ai
    • final logo.jpg
    • final logo.psd
    • final logo.svg
    • final logo.png
    Download all five files from the *Digital Technologies 7 & 8* website to your computer.
2   Open the final logo.jpg file (a bitmap-based or raster format) in an application such as Photoshop. Zoom in on the detail shown here. What do you notice?

5vs5 Football (5vs5.com.au)

Figure 2.26 Zoomed detail in logo

3   Open the final logo.svg file (a vector-based format) in a vector application such as Illustrator. Zoom in on the same detail shown above to the maximum possible. What do you notice? If you have a copy of Illustrator, open the .ai Illustrator file and inspect the layers.
4   Arrange the file names shown in step 1 in increasing order of size, and complete Table 2.9. Details of the .tif version have been entered as it is too large for download. If necessary, use an online search to discover any special features for each type.

Table 2.9

File	File size	Vector or bitmap?	Special features of file type?
Final logo.tif	*91.1 MB*	*Bitmap*	*High quality suitable for high-resolution printing*

5 Explain the reasons for differences in file size using what you learned earlier in this unit about how data is stored.

6 Collect five of your favourite images or logos. You may like to add them to a Pinterest account. Identify the file type of each.

REPRESENTING AUDIO USING BINARY

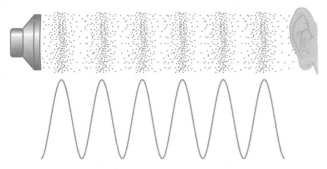

Figure 2.27 We represent analog sound using graphs, which makes most people think that sound looks like these graphs; however, it is really just vibrating air particles.

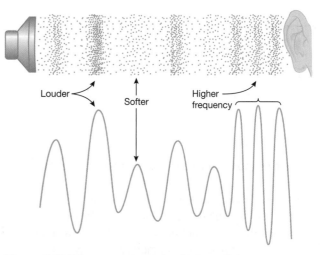

Figure 2.28 When sounds are loud, air particles are more compressed and wave height is high. When a sound is higher pitched, sound waves are closer.

Analog sound

Analog sound is a series of pressure waves in air. A microphone converts these into voltage changes on a wire so that high pressure becomes positive voltages and low pressure becomes negative voltages (Figure 2.27).

These voltages can be recorded onto tape as changes in magnetic strength of tiny particles or on old vinyl records in the form of wiggles in a groove which cause a needle to vibrate.

Loudspeakers reverse this. Changing voltages cause the speaker cone to vibrate and create air pressure waves, which vibrate our eardrums.

Digital audio

Digital audio captures sounds using only 0s and 1s. How is this done?

To digitise analog sound waves two things need to be captured: the pitch or frequency (how often the pressure waves occur), and the volume or amplitude (how strong they are) (see Figures 2.29 and 2.30).

When you record from a microphone, analog-to-digital converters (ADC) sample analog signals by taking lots of regularly spaced measurements.

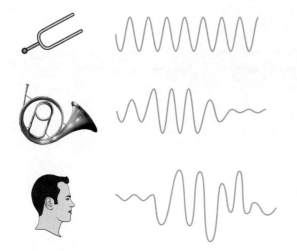

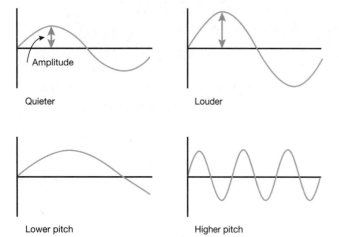

Figure 2.29 Different sounds produce different wave shapes

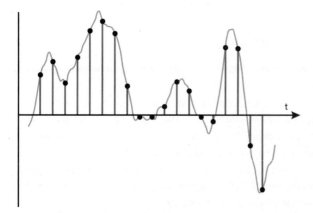

Amplitude

Quieter

Louder

Lower pitch

Higher pitch

Figure 2.30 Top: Audio volume. Bottom: Audio pitch.

Sample rate

The original waveform is broken into snapshots called samples.

The blue analog wave (Figure 2.31) is approximated by noting its values (the black dots) at regularly spaced moments. Each of these 'samples' is stored as a number measuring wave height at that moment. **Sample rate** describes the number of samples taken each second.

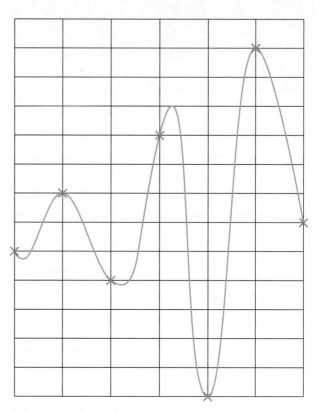

We lose all data between these samples. Imagine the audio analog sound shown in Figure 2.32.

If we digitally sample this audio signal five times over one second, then the wave would appear like the orange line in Figure 2.33. A big part of the original blue wave has been

Figure 2.32 An analog wave

t

Figure 2.31 Sampling an audio signal

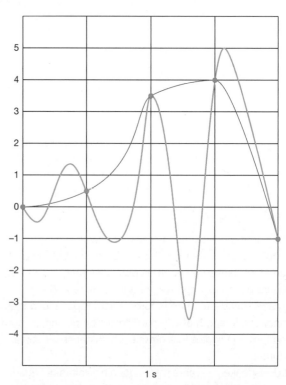

Figure 2.33 Five samples taken over one second with values 0.0, 0.5, 3.5, 4.0 and –1.0

9780170411813

missed (the big dip in the second last interval). This would be a poor approximation to the true shape, so the digitised signal would not sound like the original.

The number of samples taken per second is measured in **hertz (Hz)**. The graph shows a sample rate of 5 Hz, or five samples taken per second. MP3 music samples at 44 100 Hz (44 100 samples per second) and professional recordings use 48 000 Hz.

Web probe: MP3

Find out why such a strange number as 44 100 Hz was chosen for the MP3 standard.

_____

_____

Activity: Sampling sound

Look at Figure 2.34 showing an analog audio signal sampled seven times over one second (7 Hz). Measuring the height of the wave at each of the intervals in Figure 2.34 we get the values:

5, 7, 4, 9, 0, 12, 6

1 Convert these values to binary (the first two have been done for you).

0101, 0111, _____, _____, _____, _____, _____.

This is the new digitised audio file, entirely described by binary code.

2 If you heard it played, how close do you think it would sound to our original analog file? Give one reason for your answer.

_____

_____

_____

_____

_____

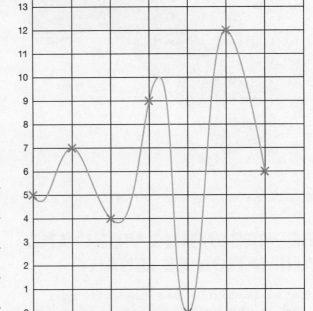

Figure 2.34 Seven samples over one second

Audio bit depth

Bit depth refers to the number of bits used for the audio samples, in the same way as it refers to the number of bits used to represent colour in images.

In the last activity a bit depth of 4 was used. That is, we had only 4 bits for our binary numbers, so only eight different numbers to use to describe height: 0101, 0111, etc.

Using only 4 bits, there is no number to represent 5.5 and it would have to round it to the nearest whole number.

If the number of bits is low, then measurements cannot be very precise and sound quality suffers. Figure 2.35 on the following page illustrates how bit depth affects sound files.

A common bit depth for audio is 16 bits, giving 65 536 (2^{16}) numbers, or different levels.

We have been discussing mono sound only. Most audio is recorded in stereo and each of the tracks needs to be recorded separately. Digital file sizes double for stereo (see Figure 2.35, next page).

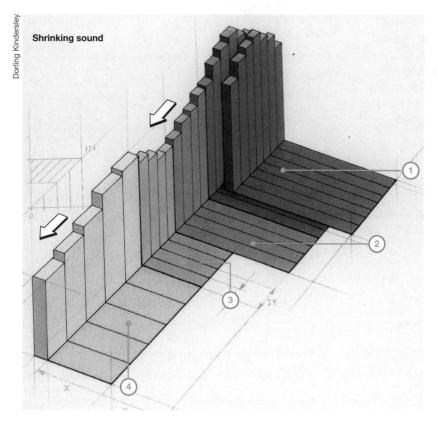

Dorling Kindersley

Shrinking sound

While most multimedia machines can play stereo CD-quality sound, many titles use lower sound quality. Sound files can be made smaller by a factor of 16 or more, but unfortunately, the quality drops too.

1 **CD-quality stereo sound** At its best, multimedia sound uses 44 100 samples a second (each sample is shown here as an upright block) and uses 16 binary digits, or bits, to measure each sample.

2 **Stereo to mono** The simplest way to shrink sound is to combine the two stereo channels, left and right, into one mono channel.

3 **Half the bits** By using 8 bits instead of 16 to measure each sample, the sound file is made smaller still, but the result is a less precise, grittier sound.

4 **Half the samples** To shrink the sound file even further, half as many samples are used every second. This makes the sound 'muddier'.

Figure 2.35 How bit depth and sample size affect sound files

REPRESENTING VIDEO AND ANIMATION AS BINARY

Video and animation files are a collection of images.

One difference between video and animation is that video begins as continuous motion broken up into a sequence of frames, whereas animators begin with separate images and display these rapidly to create the illusion of motion.

Imagine the demands of video on binary data! Video requires 25 images every second, each one around 1 megabyte (MB). The total size of a one-hour video could be 1 gigabyte (GB) and 3 GB in HD format.

These large file sizes can be a problem. If the video is an included part of a bigger file, then it can occupy a large amount of space. It is said to be embedded. An alternative is to deliver or stream only those parts of the video needed at that time. Besides streaming, compression of data can be used to reduce video file sizes. We learn more about compression in *Digital Technologies 9 & 10*.

An even greater challenge is to process each image so quickly that the movie plays smoothly, along with processing the audio!

WHICH FILE FORMAT TO USE?

The digital media types we have discussed can be stored in many ways. We call these different **file formats**. Knowledge of file formats helps avoid problems when files need to be opened using different applications or different platforms.

The file format chosen to store a graphic can be very important to a designer. A common example is a bitmap (raster) graphic designed in Photoshop. If it is to be used in a desktop publishing application for reproduction in, for example, a school magazine, then a suitable format could be TIFF (.tif), at a resolution of 300 dpi (dots per inch). If the same graphic is to be used in a web page (where standard screen resolutions are 72 dpi), a suitable choice could be JPEG (.jpg), PNG (.png) or GIF (.gif) to keep file sizes to a minimum for faster downloads. If a designer wants to edit the image again, then the file should be retained in the original Photoshop (.psd) format to preserve the separated layers in the image.

Some image files can be very large and compression can be an important technique in graphics. This is discussed in more detail in *Digital Technologies 9 & 10*.

See Table 2.10 for a list of common formats.

9780170411813

Table 2.10 Popular file formats

Animation/video	
AVI	Audio Video Interleaved. A container format for digital video and audio under Microsoft Windows; it can also be played using other operating systems.
GIF Animated	Animated Graphics Interchange format. Based on GIF, this format allows individual frames to be displayed rapidly, one after the other. Commonly used on web pages.
MOV (QuickTime)	This is a multipurpose, cross-platform container format developed by Apple that can be used with most multimedia data types. It now also forms the basis of the MPEG-4 standard.
MPEG	Moving Picture Experts Group. A standard format for storage of digital video for all major platforms. It uses high (and lossy) compression by only storing the changes between frames.
SWF (Flash)	Small web format. A popular format on the web for displaying interactive, vector-based animations with audio.
WMV	Windows Media Video. Video file compress with Windows Media compression, a format developed by Microsoft.

Audio	
AAC	Advanced Audio Coding. A compressed audio format similar to MP3, but better at handling higher frequencies.
AIFF	Audio Interchange File Format. A sound format developed by Apply that stores 8- or 16-bit sound.
MIDI	Musical Instrument Digital Interface. This stores musical data in the form of information about the musical notes and a selection from among numerous simulated instruments.
MP3	MPEG Audio Layer III. A subset of the MPEG video format and a very popular audio format that can achieve 11:1 compression of files by only storing the audible spectrum.
WAV	Waveform Audio. A sound format developed by Microsoft and IBM using 44.1 kHz (kilohertz), 16-bit, stereo format.
WMA	Windows Media Audio. Audio file compressed with Windows Media compression. A format developed by Microsoft, similar to the MP3.

Graphics	
AI	Adobe Illustrator's native format, a vector graphics editing program; composed of paths connected by points.
BMP	Bitmap. This is the default bitmapped graphic format for Microsoft Windows computers, but can also be used on other systems. They result in large files with no compression.
EPSF (or EPS)	Encapsulated PostScript® format. This is a vector graphic format.
GIF	Graphics Interchange Format. Popular lossless compression suitable for bitmapped images of line art, and images with blocks of colour. Compression can be up to 2:1.
JPEG	Joint Photographic Experts Group. A popular graphics format that used lossy compression of up to 100:1. Best for bitmapped photographs and images with continuous tones. It is commonly used on the web and in digital cameras.
PNG	Portable Network Graphics format. Lossless format created as alternative to GIF, supports transparency, widely used on the Internet.
PSD	Photoshop Document. Adobe Photoshop's native format. May include image layers, adjustment layers, layer masks.
3D formats	There are many formats used to store and exchange 3D data files, but none as yet has become an industry standard. OBJ, 3DS (used by Autodesk 3ds Max) and DAE (Collada) file formats are common.
TIF (or TIFF)	Tagged Image File Format. A popular bitmapped format for printed publications and desktop publications.
SVG	Scalable Vector Graphics. An all-purpose vector format created mainly for the web.

Text	
ASCII (TXT)	American Standard Code for Information Interchange, also known as text (TXT). The standard format for exchange of text and numerical data.
DOCX	Unlike DOC files, which store document data in a single binary file, DOCX files are created using Open XML format, and contain separate files and folders in a compressed package.

Text	
HTML	Hypertext Markup Language. A text-based language with embedded tags that indicated the locations of images, audio and other files and attributes for text and layout display.
PDF	Portable Document Format. A format owned by Adobe Systems that preserves the appearance of text and graphics across platforms.
RTF	Rich Text Format. A format based on ASCII that retains basic formatting.
Unicode	Can represent over 110 000 characters and is used to represent text written in most of the world's languages.

Research what video streaming is and how it works.

REVIEW: BINARY REPRESENTATION

Identify

1   What are two methods for representing the text data type?

_____

_____

_____

2   Name a method for digitising each of the following:
    • text in a printed document

_____

    • a real world image of a person

_____

    • a voice

_____

    • a studio artist recording

_____

3   In the loading of a website for a user, which would likely take the greatest time: text, images, audio, video or animation? Explain your answer.

_____

_____

_____

_____

_____

_____

_____

_____

_____

_____

Analyse

4 Outline a method for converting analog audio data to digital data.

_____

_____

_____

_____

_____

5 The term bit depth is used when digitising both image and audio data. Explain how the term is used in each case.

_____

_____

_____

_____

_____

6 If it takes 4 bits to record the colour of a pixel, how many bits are needed to record an image 500 pixels high by 540 pixels wide? What would be the file size in bytes for this graphic?

_____

_____

Investigate

7 Research the MIDI audio format and explain how it works. What are its strengths and limitations?

_____

_____

_____

_____

_____

_____

_____

_____

_____

_____

_____

_____

03 UNDERSTANDING PROGRAMMING USING A GENERAL-PURPOSE LANGUAGE

OUTCOMES

Australian Curriculum content descriptions:
- Investigate how digital systems represent text, image and audio data in binary (ACTDIK024) AC
- Define and decompose real-world problems taking into account functional requirements and economic, environmental, social, technical and usability constraints (ACTDIP027) AC
- Design algorithms represented diagrammatically and in English, and trace algorithms to predict output for a given input and to identify errors (ACTDIP029) AC
- Implement and modify programs with user interfaces involving branching, iteration and functions in a general-purpose programming language (ACTDIP030) AC

GLOSSARY

algorithm Step-by-step procedure to solve a problem

branching A choice between two or more possible paths in an algorithm, depending on the response to a given condition. Also known as selection

control structures Basic building blocks of a computer program. The three control structures are sequence, branching and iteration

desk checking Method used by programmers to check the logic of an algorithm to reduce the likelihood of errors occurring. This may be done on paper, using a diagram, or mentally

flowchart Pictorial method for describing a procedure or algorithm

function Part of a computer program that performs a procedure or routine. May return a value or merely perform an operation

general-purpose programming languages Programming language able to be used for many applications and purposes. Often therefore a text-based rather than a visual programming language

iteration A set of instructions in computer programming that repeats until a change of test condition ends the process. For example, the

word WHILE might be followed by a test that asks if a counter is less than some value. This test can act as a gatekeeper and only allow the program to enter the loop when the test is true. As the counter value can change the loop can eventually be escaped

sequence Set of instructions in computer programming which follow one another in order. Each instruction must be completed before the next one is executed

structured English Simplified English statements using keywords to unambiguously describe the steps of an algorithm and to assist later coding in a computer language. Also known as pseudocode

syntax Rules or grammar of a programming language

variable A storage location reserved by a program and given a name (called an identifier), which contains data (called a value)

visual programming language Program code represented as graphical blocks in place of text. For example, variously shaped blocks in jigsaw-like shapes that can only be joined in given ways, resulting in syntax error-free program code

UNDERSTANDING THE WORLD'S MOST COMPLEX MACHINE

The computer is the most complex machine humans have created and the programs that run on them can be even more complex.

You may think this would make it very difficult for you to learn to program a computer. However, no matter how complex programs are, they all depend on a small collection of basic ideas. And at their lowest level, the only thing computers really do is process two different voltages: one low and one high, which are represented by 0 and 1.

If you first learn some basic concepts, programming becomes far easier and makes more sense.

This chapter lays the foundation you need to complete the programming projects in *Digital Technologies 9 & 10*. This chapter also gets you started on our number guesser Guided Project in Chapter 6.

DESCRIBING ALGORITHMS

Computer programs depend on **algorithms**. An algorithm is a step-by-step procedure to solve a problem. If you were asked to make a cup of tea for someone, you would follow an algorithm in your head, which might involve decisions such as 'which type of tea do they like?', 'do they have sugar?' and 'do they have milk?'.

Once a programmer has created a method, or algorithm, they code it in a computer language and run it. However, they need a way to describe algorithms before they start.

Computer programmers have invented two main ways to represent algorithms. One is a pictorial method called a **flowchart** and the other a word method called **structured English**.

FLOWCHARTS

A flowchart is a pictorial method for describing a procedure or algorithm.

It uses five basic symbols (Figure 3.1).

Flowcharts always BEGIN and END with rounded shapes containing those words. Any action that needs to be performed is drawn in a rectangle. Any information (input or output) needed from a user of the program

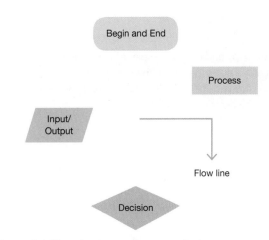

Figure 3.1 Flowcharts use these symbols

or any information given to the user is drawn in a parallelogram.

Finally, any question or decision is drawn in a diamond. These decisions always have one flowline entering them and two flowlines leaving them: one for when an answer to a decision is True and one for when it is False.

Here is a flowchart for preparing a bath (Figure 3.2). It might form the first idea for coding a program to automatically fill a bath.

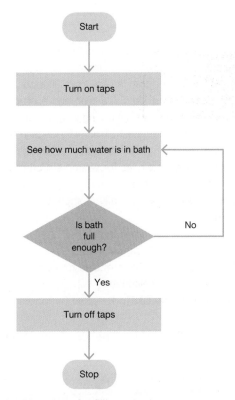

Figure 3.2 Flowchart for filling a bath

1   Photocopy and cut out the pieces shown in Figure 3.3 and arrange them on a sheet of blank paper in the correct order for making a cup of tea. Glue them in place.
2   Draw flowlines between the shapes to show correct logic and add the words 'True' and 'False' to the two flowlines coming from the decision diamonds.

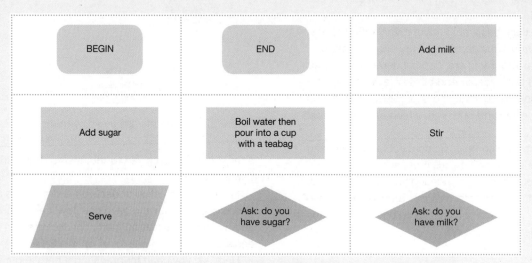

Figure 3.3 Arrange these in a flowchart describing an algorithm for making a cup of tea.

STRUCTURED ENGLISH

In addition to flowcharts, programmers invented structured English as a simple way of using words to describe an algorithm. Structured English is very much like plain English. We use it to describe the logic in a program. A programmer can easily translate this into a working program using one of many programming languages. Structured English is a form of pseudocode, which means 'not quite real code'.

There are a few simple rules for writing structured English:
*   START and END are used
*   statements are ordered logically to show execution from top down
*   logical blocks of code are indented
*   keywords are written in capital letters
*   IF, THEN, ELSE and ENDIF are used for conditional statements involving selection
*   REPEAT, WHILE, and UNTIL are used for looping or repetition.
    Study the example of structured English on the right.

```
START
IF it is raining outside THEN
  Catch the bus
ELSE
  IF it is less than 2km to destination THEN
  Walk
  ELSE IF it is less than 10km to destination THEN
  Ride a bicycle
  ELSE
  Catch the bus
  ENDIF
ENDIF
END
```

Australian Curriculum, Assessment and Reporting Authority (ACARA). 2016.
'Glossary'. The Australian Curriculum: Digital Technologies, Version 8

Imagine a number guessing game being played against a computer (Figure 3.4). The computer has secretly chosen a number (under 100) and you have to guess it as quickly as you can. How would you program a computer to play this number game?

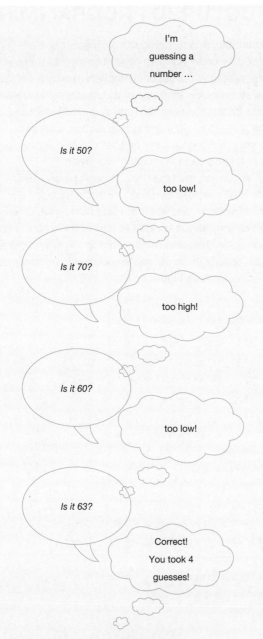

Figure 3.4 Number guessing game

Our number guessing game algorithm might look like this using Structured English:

```
BEGIN high low guessing game version 1
    set secret to 63
    get guess
    WHILE guess is not equal to secret
        IF guess > secret THEN
            print "too high"
        ELSE
            print "too low"
        ENDIF
        get next guess
    ENDWHILE
    print "correct!"
END
```

Try to understand this algorithm by tracing with your fingers while imagining the game played as in the thought bubbles to the left.

1 Cut out a copy of the pieces in Figure 3.5 and arrange them on sheet of blank paper in the correct order to represent the algorithm for this game as a flowchart.

2 Draw flowlines between these pieces to show correct logic.

3 Add 'True' and 'False' to flowlines coming from decision diamonds.

4 Finally, add in the extra symbols needed to allow the play to guess more than once and to count these guesses.

5 Carefully check through your program, by pretending secretnum (the secret number) is equal to 63.

6 Check what happens if your guess is 1, 29, 31 or 100.

7 Which method do you think you would prefer to use? – flowcharts or structured English?

_____

_____

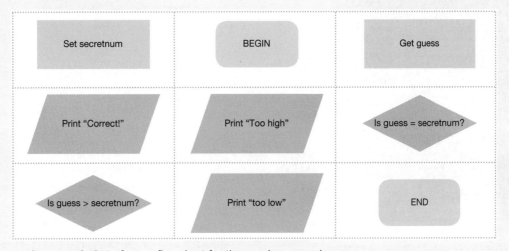

Figure 3.5 Arrange these symbols to form a flowchart for the number guessing game.

VISUAL PROGRAMMING

Many people imagine that all computer languages are difficult. This is not true.

Scratch and Blockly are great ways to learn programming. They both use a visual programming approach with jigsaw-shaped pieces that will only join up in correct ways. This eliminates a lot of errors first programmers make, known as **syntax** errors. A syntax error occurs when rules for a computer language are broken.

Visual languages are becoming very sophisticated and are being used now to perform advanced programming.

Activity: Clever kitty!

Using the free **visual programming language** Scratch, we have created our earlier number guessing program (see Figure 3.6). Try tracing through the program, noting how the logic matches our earlier versions written in structured English and as a flowchart.

Skill builder

Download Scratch (or use the online version) and recreate this game yourself.

You can find all the shapes in Scratch's Scripts left hand panel by noting their colours. You will need to create two variables, secret and guess, in Scratch's Data tab. A **variable** is just a container for holding a value. Click the green flag to run your program.

Scratch (CC-BY-SA 2.0 License (https://scratch.mit.edu/))

```
when      clicked
set  secret ▼  to  pick random 1 to 100
say  Guess my secret integer  for 2 secs
ask  What's your guess?  and wait
set  guess ▼  to  answer
repeat until  (guess) = (secret)
    if  (guess) > (secret)  then
        say  Too high!  for 2 secs
    else
        say  Too low!  for 2 secs
    ask  What's your guess?  and wait
    set  guess ▼  to  answer
play sound  meow ▼
say  You guessed it!  for 2 secs
```

Figure 3.6 Number guessing game using the visual Scratch programming environment.

STRUCTURED PROGRAMMING

Like all complex things, computer programs can be understood by breaking them down into simpler parts. A computer program is a set of instructions run by a computer, just as a storybook is made up of a collection of sentences. Computer instructions are like turn-by-turn directions you might be given: turn right at the intersection, walk two blocks, keep walking until the first set of traffic lights. The computer follows each instruction you give it.

Early languages, such as the first versions of BASIC (Beginner's All-purpose Symbolic Instruction Code), used lines of instructions, and each line was numbered. Often there were many jumps to another part of the program code and back again. This was messy, hard to follow and became known as 'spaghetti' code, and sometimes in Australia as 'kangaroo' code (See Figure 3.7).

Example of older 'spaghetti' code

```
10   INPUT "What is your name: ", U$
20   PRINT "Hello "; U$
30   INPUT "How many stars do you want: " N
40   S$ = ""
50   I = 1
55   IF I > N THEN GOTO 80
60   S$ = S$ + "*"
65   I=I+1
70   GOTO 55
80   PRINT S$
90   INPUT "Do you want more stars? ", A$
100  IF LEN(A$) = 0 THEN GOTO 90
110  A$ = LEFTS(A$, 1)
120  IF A$ = "Y" OR A$ = "y" THEN GOTO 30
130  PRINT "Goodbye "; U$
140  END
```

The same code now structured in Python

```python
UserName=input('What is your name: ')
print ('Hello ', UserName)
Answer='Y'
Numstars=1
while Answer == 'Y':
    NumStars=int(input('How many stars do you want: '))
    print (NumStars * '*')
    Answer=''
    while Answer=='':
        Answer=input( 'Do you want more stars? ')
        Answer=Answer[:1].upper()
print ('Goodbye ', Username)
```

Figure 3.7 An example of line-numbered old-style 'spaghetti' code compared to the same program written in a structured language, such as Python. This Python program prints stars on a line. If you already know a little Python, copy and test it out!

9780170411813

CONTROL STRUCTURES: BREAKING IT ALL DOWN

A Dutch computer scientist, Edsger Wybe Dijkstra, disliked the way code logic would jump around and popularised another method called structured programming using only three **control structures**.

Web probe: Blockly Maze

To discover structured programming in a fun way, try Blockly Maze. Google it and see if you can get to level 10!

No matter how complex an algorithm is, it is built using just three basic building blocks, called control structures. This is similar to the way many complex Lego structures can be built using just a few shapes.

These three control structures are **sequence**, **branching** (or selection) and **iteration** (or repetition) (see Figure 3.8).

You have used these control structures in your visual programming already.

In this unit we will cover the basics and you will be well on your way to knowing how to code.

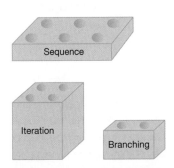

Figure 3.8 In the same way as three LEGO brick shapes can be used to create thousands of different structures, these three building blocks of computer programming (sequence, branching and iteration) can be used to create countless different programs.

Sequence

The first three lines of our example program number guessing program used a sequence. This is the simplest type of control structure and the only one the earliest computing programs used. It is just one instruction followed by the next (see Figure 3.9).

Branching (selection)

Most programs reach a point where they have to decide what to do next. In order to make the decision, the program asks a question or tests a condition. This is called the branching or selection control structure (branching and selection can be used interchangeably). The number guessing program uses selection when it asks if guess is larger or smaller than secret and delivers an appropriate message.

In a flowchart, we represent selection using a diamond-shaped box from which two flowlines emerge, one for Yes and one for No. In structured English we use the words IF, THEN, ELSE and ENDIF for selection.

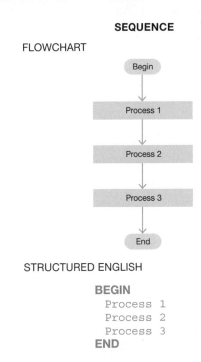

Figure 3.9 The sequence control structure in both flowchart and structured English

The selection diagram (Figure 3.10) allows a choice between two options, and is known as binary selection. Another is used when we are faced with many choices, and is known as multiple selection or multi-way selection.

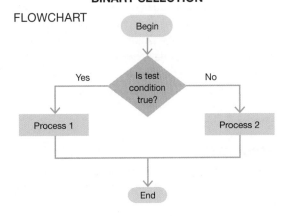

STRUCTURED ENGLISH

```
IF <text conditions> = True THEN
  do Process 1
ELSE
  Do Process 2
END IF
```

Figure 3.10 The binary selection control structure in both flowchart and structured English

In these situations, we may use the CASEWHERE (also known as SELECT CASE) structure for multi-way (multiple) branching.

In a software-driven hot drink machine (Figure 3.11) only one action will be performed.

Written in structured English:

```
CASEWHERE Drinkselected is
   Coffee:         pour coffee
   Tea:            pour tea
   Hot chocolate:pour hot chocolate
OTHERWISE:         do nothing
ENDCASE
```

Select your drink

- ⦿ Coffee
- ○ Tea
- ○ Hot Chocolate

Figure 3.11 The interface for a drink machine using multi-way selection could appear like this. Radio buttons allow only one choice to be made.

Iteration (repetition)

The third control structure in our program is iteration (also known as repetition).

In our number guesser, the word WHILE is followed by a test, which acts as a gatekeeper, comparing values of guess and secret. It only allows the program to progress if these values are not equal.

Iteration, or looping, is the most important of all the control structures as it allows a computer to repeat actions effortlessly over and over again.

The iteration structure does not have a special flowchart symbol. We use the diamond decision box to perform a test, a process rectangle for the action and a looping flowline to show that a section of code repeats.

The type of loop we decide to use depends on how we want it to behave. Two important categories of loops are:
- pre-test loops
- post-test loops.

Pre-test loop

A pre-test loop performs a test before a loop. The program may not enter the loop at all depending on the outcome of the test condition.

If we run a finger around the logic flow lines in Figure 3.12, we see that the loop tests the condition, and only executes the loop code while the condition is True, then tests the condition again, and keeps repeating this cycle until the WHILE test condition is False.

This structure is often known as a WHILE loop. In structured English it looks like this:

```
WHILE test condition is True
   do process
ENDWHILE
```

PRE-TEST LOOP

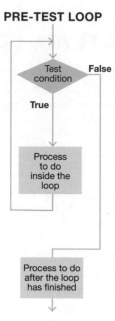

Figure 3.12 A process inside a pre-test loop is only executed if the test condition permits it.

Post-test

A post-test loop performs a test at the end of a loop. This type of loop must always perform the loop at least once – the very first time – until a test condition causes the loop to terminate. In structured English:

```
REPEAT
   do process
UNTIL test condition is True
```

If we run a finger around the logic flow lines in Figure 3.13, we can see that the loop performs the process first and only then tests the condition, repeating the loop code again if it evaluates to False, or exiting when it evaluates to True.

POST-TEST LOOP

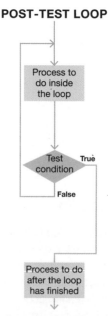

Figure 3.13 A process inside a post-test loop is always executed at least once before testing for a possible repeat.

LEARNING TO CODE USING A GENERAL-PURPOSE LANGUAGE

In this unit we move from using visual programming to general-purpose languages that are coded using special keywords and syntax rules.

Keywords and syntax can be compared to vocabularies and grammar in regular human languages. Keywords are the vocabulary of a computing language and syntax is its grammar.

This unit will introduce you to important concepts in programming, and it will give actual examples to try, but it is not a complete course in coding. To gain confidence you will need the help of your teacher in class.

Weblink

We recommend online tutorials such as: Code.org, Codecademy and Grok Learning.

Swift Playgrounds (for iPad only) is a great way to learn programming in the form of structured interactive puzzles. It teaches general principles alongside the Swift language and can even be used to control drones and robots.

Your teacher will select a particular language for your class, but whichever one you use, you will be able to transfer that knowledge easily to other computer languages (see Figure 3.14).

We have chosen the well-known language Python (version 3) for our examples because it is open-source, free, has versions for all platforms, excellent online support and tutorials, used in popular school competitions and for teaching programming in universities. Important organisations that use Python include YouTube, NASA, Google and CERN.

Using Python

Before you begin coding you need to install the latest version of Python. Follow the weblink from the *Digital Technologies 7 & 8* website.

Weblink

Your installed software features IDLE (Integrated Development and Learning Environment) used to code your programs.

Dissecting a Python!

At the beginning of this unit we used the visual language Scratch to code a number guessing game. If you were to translate this program into Python, it would look like Figure 3.15 on the following page. Even if you have never seen Python code before, see if you can understand the flow of the logic. Notice we have made a small change to include a flag to allow our program to repeat.

The red text are comments and are not part of the code. In Python, comments are preceded by the symbol #. You should get into the habit of using comments regularly to help users understand your code.

We will highlight the features of Figure 3.15.

- Indenting: Python uses indented sections to make code clearer. Indented sections create logical blocks. Other languages may use braces instead, such as { }.
- Repeat loop: The WHILE block asks if the flag is not equal to False and the whole block repeats until it is equal to False. When that happens, the program ends. We made sure the flag started equal to True in the second line of the code.
- Selection: The IF statement is indented to form a selection block. Python can also tell the program what to do if the test is false by using an else statement.

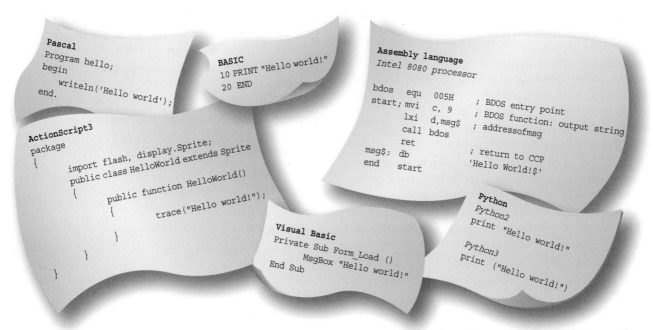

Figure 3.14 The same program written in six general-purpose computer languages. In each case, the program outputs the greeting 'Hello world!'

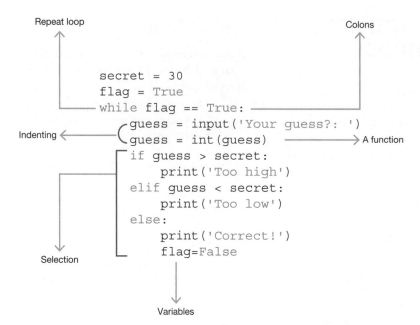

Figure 3.15 A Python version of our number guesser. Note the features of this code.

- Colons: Note how tested expressions (such as guess > secret) are followed by colons. The block after the colons is executed if the test is true.
- Functions: `input()` is a built-in Python **function** that accepts user input from the keyboard and assigns it to a variable. `print()` is a built-in Python function that will display whatever variable is placed inside its parentheses. `int(guess)` converts the guess from string to integer (whole number). If we want to print the value of a variable such as guess then we simply write its name in, e.g. `print(guess)`.
- Text strings: If we want to print a string of text, then we use single quotation marks around the string, e.g. `print('Too high')`.

Variables

All computer programs depend on the ability to store variables, like an object stored in a box. Variables are given a name (called an identifier) and contain data (called a value).

When we write `a = 3`, we are setting up space in memory that we are labelling 'a' and loading it with the value '3'. Our variable is a and its value is 3.

Many computer languages must be told in advance the type of variable (e.g. text, number, Boolean) in order to set up the correct storage. In Python all variables have to be given (assigned) a value when they are first used (declared) and their type is assigned automatically, but this means programmers need to be careful not to mix types.

In Python we assign data to a variable using the '=' sign. Python uses equal signs in two ways, each with a different meaning.

Python uses a single = for assignment of a value, as in `a = 3`. It means 'becomes'.

Python uses a double =, '==' for testing if two things are equal.

If we set

`a = 3` and `b = 4` and then type
`a==b`,

it will test if the values are equal and answer 'false'. Note no values changed.

Functions

Each programming language has built-in functions to perform common actions. These save the programmer needing to code these each time. So far our number guesser program uses these built-in Python functions: `input()`, `int()` and `print()` (see Figure 3.15).

Computer languages also allow you to create your own functions. You will learn to do this later as part of your projects.

Functions are usually written like this: `MyFunctionName()` to allow them to receive input values placed inside the parentheses.

Activity: Some equals are more equal than others!

Can you answer each 'Why?' in Figure 3.16 by explaining the output in blue following the values input in black?

```
>>> a=3          Sets value of 'a' to 3
>>> b=4          Sets value of 'b' to 4
>>> a==b
False            Why?
>>>              _____
>>> a=b          Sets value of 'a' to 'b'
>>> a==b
True             Why?
>>>              _____
```

Figure 3.16 Not all equals are equal!

9780170411813

Coding our guessing game

If you are using Python: open the IDLE Python editor. Click File > New. Type out the guessing game code exactly as you see it in Figure 3.15 and run it. In this version the secret number is always set to 30. We will improve this in the next Skill builder.

If you are not using Python, type out then run a version of the guessing game prepared by your teacher in your chosen programming language.

- Don't worry if it doesn't work the first time. This happens to nearly everyone. Computer programs only do as they are told.
- Check indentation, punctuation, spelling, capital letters.
- Ask for help if you need it.

Did you get your code working?

Skill builder

Beginner's Python essential summary

Table 3.1 Colours in the Python editor

Colour	Code element	Examples from program in Fig X

	Built-in Python functions	`print()`
		`int()`
		`input()`

	Strings	`'too high'` `'your guess'`
	Operators, numbers, variable names	`secret` `guess`

	Built-in keywords	`while`
		`if`
		`elif`
		`else`

	Comments and error messages	`# set secret number to 30`

Table 3.2 Arithmetic operators

Arithmetic operator	Symbol	Description	Example
Addition	+	Adds two numbers	`5 + 2 = 7`
Subtraction	–	The difference between two numbers	`5 - 2 = 3`
Multiplication	*	The product of two numbers	`5 * 2 = 10`
Division	/	Division of one number by another	`5 / 2 = 2.5`
Exponent	**	First number raised to the power of the second	`5**2 = 25`
Modulus	%	The remainder when two numbers are divided	`5 % 2 = 1`
Whole number division	//	Whole number division without decimal, fraction or remainder	`5 // 2 = 2`

Table 3.3 Logical operators

Logical operator	Description	Example
==	is equal to	`if num == secret:`
>	is greater than	`if num > secret:`
<	is less than	`if num < secret:`
!=	is not equal to	`if num != secret:`
>=	is greater than or equal to	`if num >= secret:`
<=	is less than or equal to	`if num <= secret:`

Common Python examples

Table 3.4 Helpful code snippets in Python 3

How to	Python code example
Assignment *This statement will create a variable called* num *and assign it a value of 4*	```num = 4```
Display output *Use the* print *keyword*	```print('Some text')```
Receive input *Use the* input *keyword*	```name = input('What is your name?')```
Convert to integer	```num = input('Enter a number: ')``` ```mynum = int(num)```
Display a message along with a variable's value	```print('Your number is',num)```

Selection: the if statement
(elif *and* else *are both optional)*
	```if num == secret:```
	``` print('Well done')```
	```elif num < secret:```
	``` print('too low')```
	```else:```
	``` print('too high')```

Import a module *Some functions need to be imported first. This one generates a random integer 1 to 100*	```import random``` ```num=random.randint(1,100)```
Iteration: the for loop	```for x in range(0,10):``` ``` print('python is cool')```
Iteration: the while loop	```while password!='python':``` ``` password=input('Enter your password: ')```

Define a function
Use def *keyword and indent.* return *keyword delivers answer*
	```def circleArea(r):```
	``` area=3.14*r**2```
	``` return area```

Call a function *This calls the function above and provides a value for the radius 'r'*	```circleArea(4)```

Adding a random function

We want our program code to generate a random number. There is a function in most languages to do this. We will use Python in these examples. In Python the collection of random number functions is called, not surprisingly, *random*. Some functions need to be imported as they are not available automatically so we first import the random number module in our first line of code:

```
import random
```

We want to create random integers. This is a function called randint(). Because randint is part of the random module, we refer to it this way:

```
random.randint(1,100)
```

This generates random integers from 1 to 100.

Skill builder: Version 2

Adding a function to our guessing game

Let's improve version 1 of our guessing game code by adding the random function explained above. This one generates a new random secret number each time the program is run. This version is written in Python. Your teacher will help you if you use another language.

We will also print our secret number to help us debug. Replace

```
secret = 30
```

with (see Table 3.4)

```
import random
num=random.randint(1,100)
print(secret)
```

Figure 3.17 on the next page shows how Version 2 will now appear.

9780170411813

```
import random
secret = random.randint(1,100)
print(secret)
flag = True
while flag == True:
  guess = input('Your guess?: ')
  guess = int(guess)
  if guess < secret:
    print('Too low')
  elif guess > secret:
    print('Too high')
  else:
    print('Correct!')
    flag=False
```

Figure 3.17

Activity: Basics of input and output

1   Write a program to display the word "Hello" on the screen.
2   Modify the program to ask for certain data and then display it as part of a sentence, like this:

    Hello! I know a lot about you! You are
    < first name> <family name> – your
    favourite singer is <favourite
    singer> and <favourite movie actor>
    is your favourite movie actor.

3   Write a program function to calculate the area of a circle (area = πr^2). Include it in a program that asks the user for the radius of a circle in millimetres, and outputs the area of the circle.
4   Write a program to print a times table chosen by a user.
5   Write a program to print all times tables from 1 to 12.

The programming design cycle

Programming follows these four stages:
- Defining: develop and record the nature of the problem and its requirements.
- Designing: develop and test algorithms for the problem and the user interface.
- Implementing: write the code and refine it.
- Evaluating: measure the result against user needs and the goals defined at the beginning.
  You'll learn more about this in Chapter 5.

FINDING AND FIXING ERRORS

Debugging syntax errors

A syntax error is made when your code breaks the rules for the language you are using.

Punctuation may be missing, indentation incorrect, the wrong word used or used in the wrong order.

```
import random
secret = random.randint(1,100)
print(secret)
flag = True
while flag == True:
  guess = input('Your guess?: ')
  if guess < secret:
    print('Too low')
  elif guess > secret
    print('Too high')
  else:
    print('Correct!')
    flag=false
```

Figure 3.18

The errors are:

_____

_____

_____

Debugging logic errors

Logic errors are mistakes made in an algorithm by a programmer. The program runs but the answers may not be correct. Because of this such errors can be more difficult to locate. A wrong number of loops may be specified, or an incorrect formula used.

Skill builder: Version 4

A thorough desk check is vital in identifying logic errors.

Here are three versions of our guessing game. Each one has a single logic error.

Copy and run them, identify the error of logic and explain the reason it produces incorrect output.

Correct each error and for each describe its effect on the running of the program.

```
import random
secret = random.randint(1,100)
print(secret)
flag = True
while flag == True:
  guess = input('Your guess?: ')
  guess = int(guess)
  if guess > secret:
    print('Too high')
  elif guess < secret:
    print('Too low')
  else:
    print('Correct!')
    flag=False
```

Figure 3.19

```
import random
secret = random.randint(1,100)
print(secret)
flag = True
while flag == True:
  guess = input('Your guess?: ')
  guess = int(guess)
  if guess < secret:
    print('Too high')
  elif guess > secret:
    print('Too low')
  else:
    print('Correct!')
    flag=False
```

Figure 3.20

```
import random
secret = random.randint(1,100)
print(secret)
flag = True
while flag == False:
  guess = input('Your guess?: ')
  guess = int(guess)
  if guess > secret:
    print('Too high')
  elif guess < secret:
    print('Too low')
  else:
    print('Correct!')
    flag=True
```

Figure 3.21

TAKING IT FURTHER

Getting a program to run successfully often takes lots of attempts before a program runs properly, even when you have the right idea for your algorithm.

Remember that a person learning a human language for the first time will make all sorts of embarrassing errors, but usually someone listening can work out what they mean. Computers are far less intelligent. They only understand if we use exactly the right words, in the right order and with perfect punctuation! However, with advances in artificial intelligence this may not always be the case.

Skill builder: modifications

Here are ideas for modifications you can make to your number guessing program. This time you are on your own.

- Modify code to allow replays by asking for input from player.
- Keep a record of the fewest guesses each time and display it each replay.
- Prevent guesses outside the range 1–100.
- Ask for a player's name and include it in messages.
- Allow players to set range from which to guess.
- Prevent entries that are not integers (e.g. words).

In the project section there are some fun programming projects where you will extend your skills. The guided project in Chapter 6 is a great place to start as it extends the number guessing program you have just coded.

UNDERSTANDING NETWORKS

04

OUTCOMES

Australian Curriculum content descriptions:
- Investigate how data is transmitted and secured in wired, wireless and mobile networks, and how the specifications affect performance (ACTDIK023) **AC**

WHAT DOES DATA LOOK LIKE ON A NETWORK?

In this unit we will be learning how data is transmitted between computers over wired **networks** (Figure 4.1). In *Digital Technologies 9 & 10* we will learn about wireless networks.

Computers share data over complex worldwide networks, but what does this data look like and how does it get to the correct destination?

We hear so often about 0s and 1s that many people think numbers are actually being sent between networked computers. This is not true.

If the communication is over copper wire, low and high voltages are used to represent 0 and 1. If it is radio waves then the 0s and 1s can be represented using two different heights (amplitude) on the wave (AM or Amplitude Modulation) or by using two different frequencies for the wave (FM or Frequency Modulation). If it is light along glass optical fibre, then levels of light intensity are used.

Table 4.1 Media and methods for data transmission

Data transmission types	Bit represented as	
Network cable	Voltage high or low	1 0 1 1 0 1 0 1
Fibre-optic cable	Change in phase or intensity of light	Modulated wave
Radio waves	AM – varying the amplitude (height) of the wave FM – varying the frequency of the wave	AM FM

Watch the video 'Wires, cables and WFi' produced by code.org.

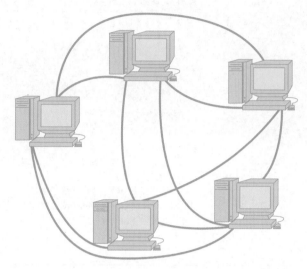

Figure 4.1 Direct cable connection between computers soon becomes impractical! We'll need some mathematics!

WIRED NETWORKS AND THE INTERNET

How computers are connected over networks

Imagine you are suddenly transported to the early days of personal computers last century and needed to share data.

Your first idea might be the simplest: connect a storage device, copy the data on to it and plug it into the other computer. You would soon get tired of connecting and reconnecting. You might also want to connect more than just two computers.

You decide to create the world's first network, but how do you do it?

The most obvious answer would be to connect each computer to each other computer using cables. Your first problem is that the earliest personal computers had no cables or even ports. But imagine you solved this.

How many cables would be needed to connect five computers in a network if each was connected to every other one? What about for 10 computers?

The following activity will show you how impossible it would be to have this many cables running between computers – especially over long distances!

Another problem would be making sure two computers did not try to communicate at the same time, causing data collisions. A different solution has to be found! These were the kinds of problems the first network designers had to solve.

Activity: Networks and handshakes

Here is a table where each row shows a number of computers with each one connected to every other one. Examine Table 4.2, complete the empty spaces and fill in the pattern for the number of cables.

Table 4.2 How many connections are there?

Network	Computers	Cables needed	Pattern	Triangular number
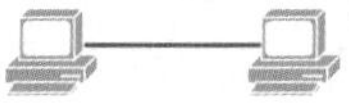	2	1	•	1
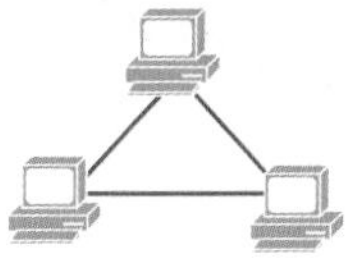	3	3	• • •	3
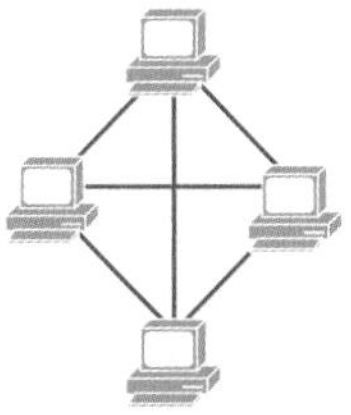	4	6	• • • • • •	6
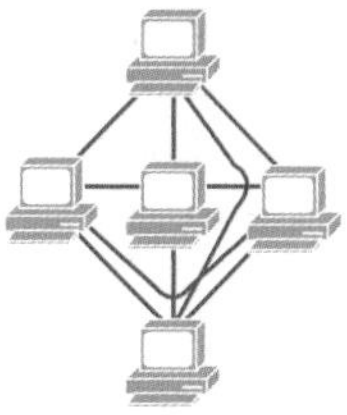	5	10	• • • • • • • • • •	10
	6			
	7			

The secret is triangular numbers. Arranging dots in triangular patterns creates triangular numbers. Each triangular pattern has one more row added to the one above. It is interesting that triangular numbers also give the total number of handshakes possible between people. Try it!

1 How many cables would be needed for 10 computers? Find the pattern in the right hand column of the table to answer this.

____

____

____

2 Can you create a spreadsheet which produces the first 100 results? Figure 4.2 shows what the first lines will look like.

	A	B
1	Number of computers	Cables
2	2	1
3	3	3
4	4	6
5	5	10
6	6	15
7	7	21
8	8	28

Figure 4.2 Spreadsheet to calculate connections if all computers are connected to each other.

First try it yourself then read these hints if you need them:

In column A fill in the numbers of computers from 2 to 101. (One computer by itself doesn't need a cable!). In cell B2 write the number `1`. In cell B3 write the formula `=SUM(B2+A2)` then Fill Down.

3 Explain how the spreadsheet 'guesses' the correct formula for each row.

____

____

____

____

4 How many cables would be needed to connect 100 computers?

____

Hubs

An early networking solution was to connect all the computers to a central device, called a **hub**.

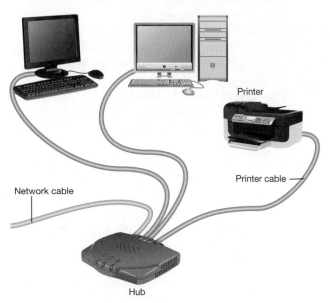

Figure 4.3 A hub is a small device that connects several network devices.

When a hub receives a message it transmits it to all the linked computers.

Hubs also act as repeaters. A repeater strengthens signals travelling over large distances. The problem with a hub is that it is likely to cause even more collisions between data than direct connections, because all the computers can transmit at the same time (Figure 4.4).

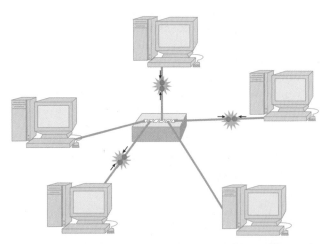

Figure 4.4 Computers can transmit to the hub at the same time, which means data collisions are likely to occur.

Switches

A network **switch** (Figure 4.5) possesses an important advantage over a hub. A switch can look at an address being sent to it and identify the correct destination port or computer, rather than transmitting it to all connected computers as a hub does.

Figure 4.5 A switch

A switch dramatically reduces the problem of data collisions as these now only occur when a computer and its switch try to talk to each other at the same time. If this happens the collision is detected and retransmitted after a short delay.

Switches have now largely replaced hubs in networks.

Switches work by keeping a table of addresses for each connected device. Each device has its own network interface card (NIC) (Figure 4.6) that is numbered with a media access control address, known as a **MAC address** (not related to the computer brand). MAC addresses are also known as **Ethernet** addresses.

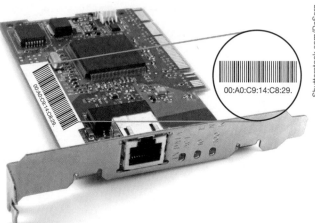

Figure 4.6 A network card

Connecting computers with switches solves the problem of a room of computers needing to communicate, or even a couple of rooms. But how do we communicate with a computer in another building, city or country? How does our switch know which of billions of connected devices it needs to connect to?

9780170411813

Routers

This problem is solved by **routers**. Routers (Figure 4.7) keep track of which device a data package has come from as well as the device it should send it to next, based on stored MAC (Ethernet) addresses. We will find out how a little later.

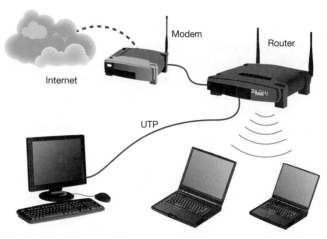

Figure 4.8 A home wireless router can provide access to the Internet for several computers.

Figure 4.7 Typical wired router

The most familiar type of routers connect the devices in your home to the Internet, through an Internet Service Provider (ISP).

Routers may be wired or wireless. You probably have a wireless router in your classroom.

There are also powerful routers connecting cities and countries at high speed along the fibre-optic cables of the Internet.

The Internet is made up of nearly 50 billion interconnected devices. How do routers perform what seems the impossible task of sending a message quickly and accurately and choosing the best device to send it to for its next hop in the journey? In the next section we will see how this problem was solved by packet switching.

Figure 4.9 Typical wireless router

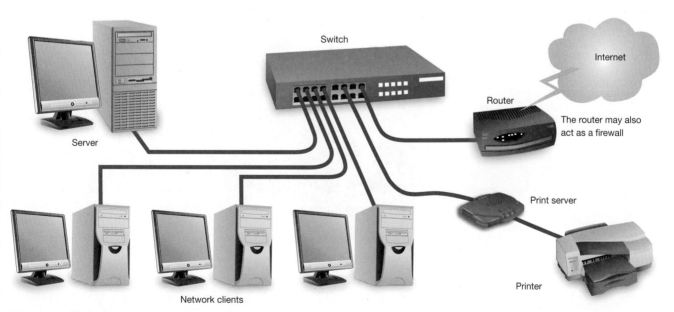

Figure 4.10 Typical network for a small business

Packet switching

A clever approach was invented to get messages to the right place quickly, even when a link is down.

By 1961, several people were working on the idea of using many routes to a destination, rather than just one. This is like our road system, where detours are possible if a section of road is out of action or busy. This idea was considered important if a nuclear war destroyed sections of the communication network. By 1973, Vint Cerf and Bob Kahn had the final concept, which became known as **Transmission Control Protocol (TCP)**. It uses a method known as **packet switching**.

Packet switching splits messages into small 'packets', transmitting each one along the best available route (using routers) and assembling them at the other end in the correct order.

Packet switching is like sending a long sentence using many postcards with one word on each, at different times and all to the same address. These might each take different postal routes and arrive at different times, but once the last one arrives, the recipient can order them correctly.

Communicating using packets instead of circuits has been one of the biggest advances in networking.

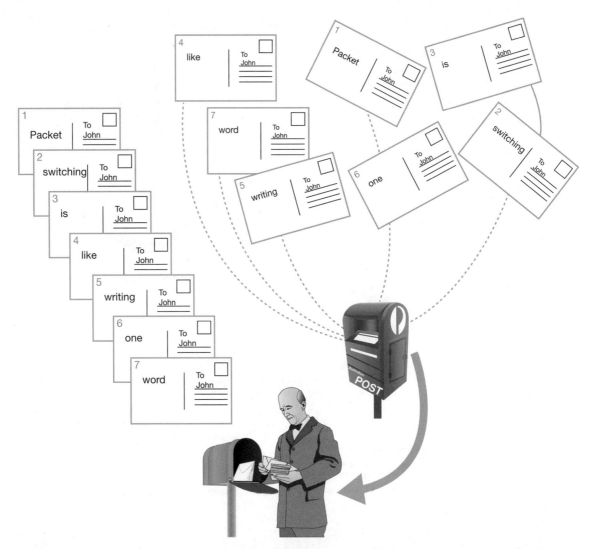

Figure 4.11 Packet switching is like sending numbered postcards with one word on each.

9780170411813

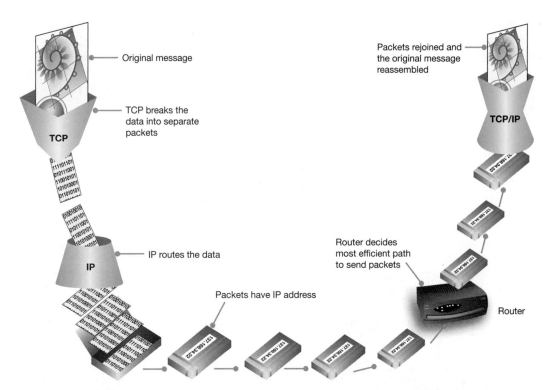

Original message

TCP breaks the data into separate packets

TCP

IP routes the data

IP

Packets have IP address

Packets rejoined and the original message reassembled

TCP/IP

Router decides most efficient path to send packets

Router

Figure 4.12 A message is divided into separate packets to send over the Internet and is rejoined at the receiving end.

What is Ethernet?

Ethernet is just one of many ways to connect computers, but it is the world's most popular. It describes a method for linking computers, sending data and checking for collisions.

To check for collisions, it uses CSMA/CD. This stands for Carrier Sense Multiple Access/Collision Detection, which makes sure two computers do not try to send packets over the network at the same time. If they are doing so, then each waits a random amount of time and tries again.

Media for wired networking

Networked computers depend upon both wired and unwired connections. Unwired connections use satellites and microwave towers. Here we summarise the common physical media used to connect computers in wired networks.

Unshielded twisted pair cable

The word Ethernet is used informally to describe the familiar blue cables that connect computers, properly known as UTP or unshielded twisted pair cables.

UTP cables have four twisted pairs of copper wires (see Figure 4.13) to reduce signal interference between wires. They are often referred to as Cat 5 or Cat 6 cables. These are used to connect each computer to a hub, switch or router. Most offices are now built with this cabling installed to wall outlets.

Standard UTP cabling can support 100 Mbps (megabits) and Gigabit Ethernet can support 1000 Mbps.

An RJ45 connector for UTP cable. This is a standard type of connector for network cards.

UTP cables contain four twisted pairs of wires, each pair twisted around the others like a rope, to reduce interference with the signal on the wire. Each wire is colour-coded to make it easy to assemble the RJ45 connectors.

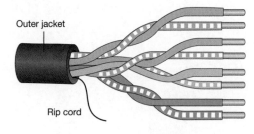

Outer jacket

Rip cord

Figure 4.13 Unshielded twisted pair cables connect easily to other network devices with the RJ45 connector.

Optical fibre

Optical fibres use light pulses over glass fibres. These allow faster transmission over longer distances than UTP cables. They also allow multiple signals to travel over the one fibre by using many wavelengths of light.

Each fibre has a thin flexible glass thread, the diameter of a human hair, which is wrapped inside another transparent surface that reflects light pulses back into this central core.

Figure 4.14 Fibre optic cable

Network speed and quality

The quality of your Internet connection is measured using 'ping', 'jitter' and 'packet loss' testing tools.

A ping measurement tells you how long it takes a packet of data to travel from your computer to a server on the Internet and back. The smaller, the better. A result below 100 milliseconds should be expected from any decent broadband connection. Jitter is the difference between two ping measurements.

If data packets are lost, this can mean much slower download and upload speeds, poor quality audio, pauses with streaming media such as video and time warping in games.

Watch the code.org videos 'Packets, routing and reliability' and 'The Internet: IP addresses and DNS'.

HOW DATA FINDS ITS WAY OVER THE INTERNET

We still haven't explained how routers know where to send their packets.

DNS

Your computer and all servers on the Internet are assigned unique addresses, known as **Internet Protocol (IP)** addresses which look like this: 216.58.212.99.

When you type www.google.com.au into your browser, a **Domain Name Server (DNS)** has the job of converting this written URL into its correct matching numerical IP address for the computer. This is done because remembering numbers is a difficult task for humans.

TCP/IP

It's time to trace a journey taken by a data packet over the Internet.

To communicate using the Internet over an Ethernet connection, a combination of protocols is used. The main ones are Transmission Control Protocol (TCP), Internet Protocol (IP), DNS (Domain Name Server) and Ethernet protocol. The first two form the well-known combination known as TCP/IP.

Imagine you type a search term into Google using your browser and hit return. Your router sends a request to the DNS to translate the URL to its corresponding IP address, 216.58.212.99.

Based on the application you used (a web browser), TCP protocol decides which port to use to communicate. Different applications 'listen' for data on different ports. These are not physical ports but codes attached to the data. Here we are using HTTP (Hypertext Transfer Protocol, through a web browser) so we would use port 80. An email sent by SMTP (Simple Mail Transfer Protocol) will be expected on port 25.

TCP now breaks the message into smaller packets, as learned earlier.

The IP address in this example is www.google.com.au. Try typing 216.58.212.99 in a browser.

Your computer knows the IP address and port to send the data. Your own computer's IP address is included to allow a response and it wraps the TCP packet inside this IP data packet.

It is like these Russian dolls (Figure 4.15) that fit inside one another.

Figure 4.15 Data packets are wrapped in protocol layers in the same way these Russian dolls fit inside each other.

Having packets with ports and IP addresses still does not help in knowing which router is next.

Based on the final IP address of your IP package, each router along the journey knows the best hop to select. For example, if the destination IP address was another capital city then a main router in your city knows the routers to the next city and so on. So your data is now wrapped in another layer containing your unique device MAC address, or Ethernet address, the MAC address for the next router as well as the maximum number of hops along the Internet allowed. It finds these correct device addresses by referring to tables it keeps updating.

Your data can now be sent in binary form over the next hop. Each router strips off the last device address (which it does not need any more), adds its own and that of the next hop.

In this way the IP addressing information in the inside packet remains the same but the destination device addresses change every hop until it reaches its final destination IP address, in this case Google's server (see Figure 4.16).

At the receiving computer, the wrappers are removed in reverse order by the protocols (again, just like Russian dolls) and TCP reassembles the separate packets in their correct order. The message has been delivered.

TCP/IP also takes care of lost packets. Each packet is given a TTL (Time to Live) number. This is an integer stating the maximum number of hops allowed, otherwise a packet could loop around the Internet forever!

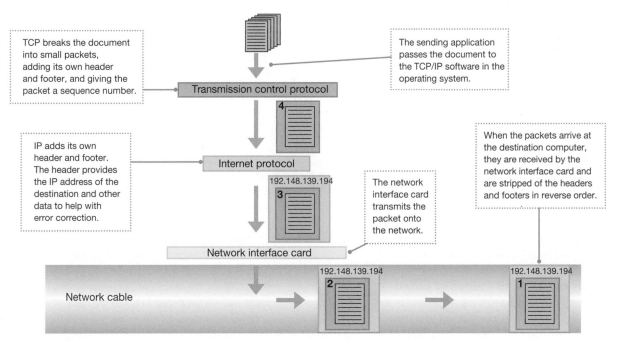

Figure 4.16 TCP/IP protocol is now built into most operating systems. Data packets 1–4 follow each other through the protocol layers.

You need

- five students (one playing a blue computer, one playing a red computer, three playing separate routers)
- six toilet rolls (three coloured blue, three coloured red, each numbered 1–3)
- a ball of string
- scissors to cut the yarn.

Aim: To be first to deliver a three-word message, which the receiving computer must reassemble and read aloud.

Both red and blue computers must flip three rolls along strings to routers, which forward them to the other computer where they are reassembled to decipher a three-word message.

Rules

- One student is elected to be the blue computer and is given three numbered red toilet rolls. Another is the red computer and given three numbered blue toilet rolls. The three other students are elected as routers.
- All students stand apart. Both *computer* students hold three lengths of string each reaching to one of the three *router* students.
- The router students each hold four strings, which reach to the four other students (including both computers).
- Blue computer sends red roll number one along a string to any router. At the same time red computer sends blue roll number one along a string to any router.
- Routers forward messages to computers of identical colour by flipping each toilet roll along the string as quickly as possible.
- Only one roll on one string at any time! If a string has a message already on it, then it must not be used and another route must be found.
- If there is a collision, then messages must go back to the senders.

How is this like TCP/IP?

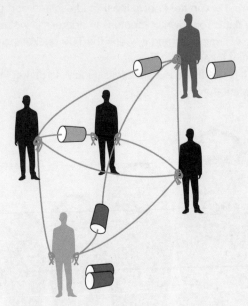

Figure 4.17 A human network

_____

_____

_____

Knowledge probe: A data packet journey

Knowledge
Probe

As outlined above, TCP/IP is a combination of two separate protocols: Transmission Control Protocol (TCP) and Internet Protocol (IP).

Perhaps the best way to explain TCP/IP is to compare it to posting a registered parcel. A signature is required from the receiver when it is delivered.

Parcel delivery can only be achieved using many short deliveries (walking, trucks, planes, etc.), which add to the total journey. In computing, which delivery hop to make next (i.e. which router and MAC number) is worked out by repeatedly referring to the written address (IP address). The street post box and the nearest sorting warehouse are like the first hop of the journey.

When drivers empty the street post box where parcels are posted, they do not take any notice of the different addresses (like the IP addresses) on them. All they need

is the location of the next sorting warehouse (the MAC address of the next router).

Sorters in the warehouse now separate parcels into local and overseas, by referring to written (IP) addresses and then into regions. They use the location of the next warehouse (like the MAC address of the next router).

When the postie finally delivers the parcel, the person's name is checked. When the actual person named in the address signs to receive the parcel, it is like the data arriving at a correct IP address by matching it to a final MAC address.

Each step in the delivery only needed a written address (IP address) to work out where to make the next hop using local knowledge for the locations (MAC addresses) of warehouses and post offices. This is like using MAC addresses to identify the next appropriate router for a data packet on an Internet journey.

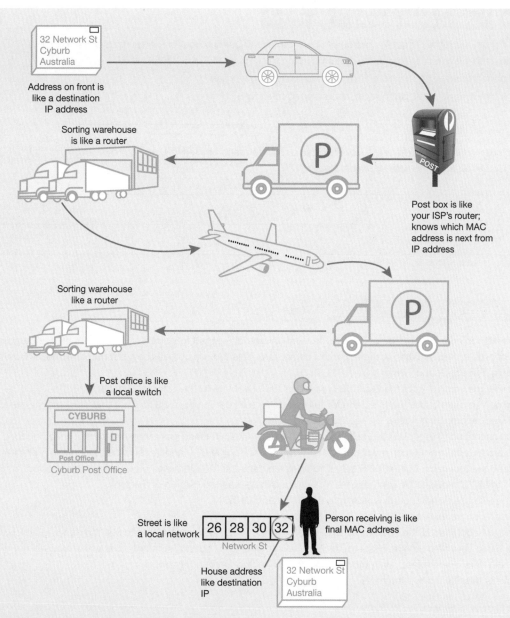

Figure 4.18 Understanding a packet's journey over the Internet

Write a summary in your own words of the way in which packet switching, routers, IP addresses and MAC addresses work to provide communication over the Internet.

_____

_____

_____

_____

_____

_____

_____

Web probe: Tracing a packet around the world

Weblink

1 Follow the weblink from the *Digital Technologies 7 & 8* website to use the YouGetSignal visual trace tool. The tool draws on a world map the journey taken by data packets to any URL you provide.

2 Enter a URL such as www.google.com and test it out using 'proxy trace'.

3 How many kilometres does the data travel, according to this tool?

_____

4 The site includes an explanation of the technique that uses information called TTL. In your own words, explain what TTL is and how it is used to trace the data packet journey.

_____

_____

_____

Class activity: Using an Internet simulator

Weblink

Code.org has designed an excellent free online Internet simulation tool (widget) to visualise, experiment with and solve different kinds of problems associated with networked computers. This tool was created by computer engineers from Microsoft, Google, Facebook and Twitter.

Teachers: Follow the weblink from the *Digital Technologies 7 & 8* website for the Internet Simulator.

Click the 'Try now' orange button on this page for full instructions on setting up a class. Note that students' names can be entered in one step by preparing names on separate lines.

Students: You cannot use this tool by yourself. It simulates a network so it needs more than one person linked up for it to work!

Once names are entered, your teacher will provide the class with a single URL and passwords. Your name represents your domain name and the tool has a built-in DNS server to translate names to IP addresses on this simulated network.

1 Login using the URL provided by your teacher. You will use the advanced version of the tool.

2 Click on the radio button next to the words: Internet Simulator: DNS.

3 Click to join one of the routers.

4 Examine the network map at the top left of the Simulator window. You will only be able to see the router to which you are connected, along with other users of that router. You will see your DNS but not those of other users. You will not be able to see any other users in your class, even though they are connected to your network.
In what ways is this like the real Internet?

_____

_____

_____

5 Use the DNS server to find the IP address of another user of your router. The DNS server will respond if you ask in the correct way. You can request the IP address of anyone in your class, even if they're connected to a different router!

6 Type the IP address of the DNS into the 'To' field, then use the following protocol to retrieve the IP address of another user (Figure 4.19):

        GET <hostnameOfPerson>

For example: GET cv9

Once you've sent your request, DNS responds with the hostname and IP address (Figure 4.20).

Figure 4.19 Using GET instruction to ask DNS for IP address of user cv9

Figure 4.20 IP address 1.13 is received for user cv9

7 After DNS has returned the user's IP, you can contact them directly by typing the IP address into the 'To' field, entering a message, and then pressing 'send' (Figure 4.21).

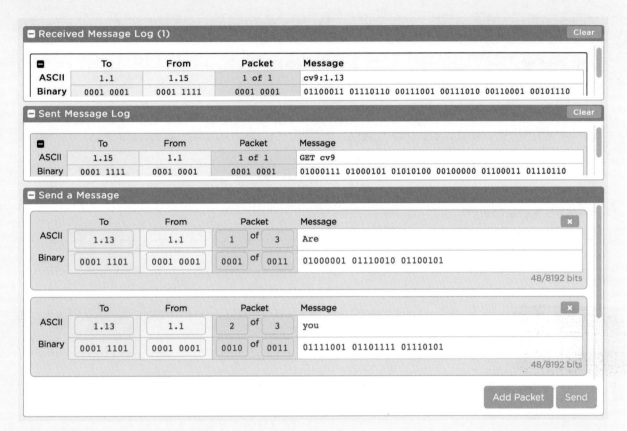

Received Message Log (1)   Clear

	To	From	Packet	Message
ASCII	1.1	1.15	1 of 1	cv9:1.13
Binary	0001 0001	0001 1111	0001 0001	01100011 01110110 00111001 00111010 00110001 00101110

Sent Message Log   Clear

	To	From	Packet	Message
ASCII	1.15	1.1	1 of 1	GET cv9
Binary	0001 1111	0001 0001	0001 0001	01000111 01000101 01010100 00100000 01100011 01110110

Send a Message

	To	From	Packet	Message	✕
ASCII	1.13	1.1	1 of 3	Are	
Binary	0001 1101	0001 0001	0001 of 0011	01000001 01110010 01100101	
					48/8192 bits

	To	From	Packet	Message	✕
ASCII	1.13	1.1	2 of 3	you	
Binary	0001 1101	0001 0001	0010 of 0011	01111001 01101111 01110101	
					48/8192 bits

Add Packet   Send

Figure 4.21 Now their IP is known, messages can be sent to user cv9.

8 Complete Table 4.3 by finding the IP addresses for five other users.

Table 4.3

Name	IP address
Your name	
1	
2	
3	
4	
5	

9 You will be assigned a partner. (The teacher randomly assigns a partner to each class member by drawing names out of a hat.)
You have already learned that in the actual Internet, long messages are split into packets. The Internet Simulator allows you to do this. Each packet is labelled with a sequence number and the total number of packets.

10 First find the address of your partner using DNS.

11 Decide on a question to ask, remembering that each word must be sent as a separate packet.
Any user being asked a question must wait until all the packets making up the question have arrived and only then reply to the correct sender, again using one word per packet.

12 Record the conversation in Table 4.4.

Table 4.4

Partner's name	Partner's address
Your question	**Response**
Partner's question	**Response**

13 How is this like the Internet?

_____

_____

REVIEW

Identify

1 What is a difference between a hub and a switch?

_____

_____

2 What is the purpose of a router in networking?

_____

_____

3 Identify two types of media capable of joining computers in a network.

_____

Analyse

4 Outline two advantages of packet switching.

_____

_____

5 Explain the purpose of TTL as part of TCP/IP.

_____

_____

Investigate

6 Find five locations where international data cables arrive on land in Australia.

_____

_____

9780170411813

UNDERSTANDING PROJECT MANAGEMENT

05

OUTCOMES

Australian Curriculum content descriptions:
- Plan and manage projects that create and communicate ideas and information collaboratively online, taking safety and social contexts into account (ACTDIP032)

defining Stage of the design process in which the project is investigated, understood, described and broken down into smaller tasks

design process Defining, designing, implementing and evaluating by collaborating and managing to create a digital solution

designing Stage of the design process in which the project ideas are generated, prototypes developed, algorithms prepared and user interfaces planned

evaluating Stage of the design process in which the project is measured against given criteria such as user needs and stated requirements

implementing Stage of the design process in which the project is built

project management Overall oversight and control of planning, monitoring and execution of a project. Critical features of project management are successfully achieving the stated outcomes within budget and within time

prototype Agreed set of rules controlling interaction between systems or individuals. In information systems, networking and data communication protocols determine agreed ways in which data is packaged, transmitted and exchanged

WHAT IS PROJECT MANAGEMENT?

All projects, no matter how large or small, are designed to meet a need of some kind.

The projects you undertake in this course will teach you a great many things about that topic. However, an even more valuable lesson will be what you learn about **project management**. The skills you learn will be useful for many activities in your life: from planning a holiday, making a large purchase, preparing for important exams or managing a birthday party.

You will need to consider costs, assess and manage risks, make decisions, control quality, evaluate processes, collaborate and communicate.

After the project is completed, you need to consider whether it meets the initial need and is innovative. Also ask what future risks it may face. Is it sustainable?

Consider how some software needed to adapt to touch-based input methods. Others, including Microsoft Office products, moved to the cloud and added collaborative tools.

Project management involves planning, organising and checking timelines, activities and resources. Each person has different strengths and weaknesses and different personalities. Some of us are happy to let others lead us, while others like to lead. Some may like to lead too much, and others may like to stay in the background too much!

Most technology projects require many people to succeed. They require specialist abilities and knowledge to build them. The projects you complete will help teach you how to work with others to reach a goal. This is never easy!

The importance of good communication

Figure 5.1 The projects you work on will teach you how to work with others to reach a goal.

Communication is the most important skill you will learn. Project management involves the skills of collaborating and communicating with others. This can involve verbal, written and graphical (e.g. sketches, storyboards, mind maps) communication among the project team and between the team and users.

Project team members need to keep in touch with one another. Collaborative apps such as Google Docs, Forms and Sheets can be used. Many software projects such as video games have been entirely produced without the team members ever meeting in person. Social networking is used to coordinate activities using Facebook, Twitter, blogs and wikis.

You will also complete some projects by yourself, but most will involve collaboration in a group. Some will be simple and others quite complex.

THE DESIGN PROCESS

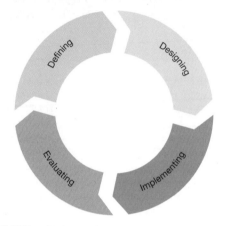

Figure 5.2 The design process

Your projects will move through the **design process**. This process starts by **defining** a problem or need, moves on to **designing** a solution, then **implementing** it and finally **evaluating** it. It is a cycle, as projects can always be improved by repeating these steps (Figure 5.2).

Although you will find it helpful to understand the separate stages of the design process, developing any project is a creative venture.

Stages of the cycle may be repeated before you reach your final product. You should celebrate unexpected discoveries; they may even send you back to re-defining the original task.

Defining

During the defining stage the project is understood, described and broken down into smaller tasks. Many project teams do not spend enough time understanding a problem or the needs it is meant to fulfil. The most common fault is a project team that thinks they understand what users want, but has not really understood the concept properly. See the cartoon (Figure 5.3) on the next page!

Most projects can be broken down into smaller ones.

For example, a game may be broken down into characters, collisions, movements and scoring.

The project manager makes a list of all tasks to be completed. You will be given a start and end time for your projects. Use these to plan a timeline.

You should think about limitations: time, technical ability, equipment, cost and social, legal and ethical issues.

When you build a project team you will need to assign roles to the team members.

Project manager

Responsible for coordinating the project and the team, reporting to the users and providing regular updates to the teacher.

Time manager

Responsible for helping the team remain on task and on schedule.

Quality manager

Responsible for identifying problems, getting resources, user interface, making sure the standard of the work is high and that all accessibility and ethical issues are met.

Communication manager

Responsible for keeping track of the project, making sure members are communicating effectively and documenting the project.

However, these main roles are not the only ones team members do. Other roles depend on the type of project and may include: designers, programmers, builders and testers.

Defining can involve these activities:
- writing a task statement
- identifying users or audience
- identifying user needs
- breaking down the problem
- developing a timeline
- listing resources
- considering social, legal and ethical issues
- assigning team roles.

Designing

Designing is the creative phase of the cycle. During this stage, ideas are generated and sketched (such as storyboards), mock-ups or **prototypes** are developed, algorithms are prepared and user interfaces are planned. A great tool for this can be a mind-mapping tool such as FreeMind or MindNode (Mac).

You should produce a prototype. A prototype is an early non-functioning version of the final product. It gives the author and the audience an idea of what the final project might look like. It is valuable as it identifies problems early on. If the project involves a user interface, its design takes place during this stage.

A great idea is to use Post-it notes to track progress. Place these next to names and/or tasks. Then use Post-it notes in traffic light colours (red, orange, green) against these to show if that task is:
- Red: failing or seriously behind time
- Orange: running into problems
- Green: on track.

Designing involves:
- generating ideas
- developing prototypes
- drawing IPO charts
- drawing flowcharts and write algorithms
- developing a user interface
- checking with users.

Activity: Projects must meet the needs of the users

Figure 5.3

What common problem faced by project teams is captured in this cartoon?

_____

_____

Implementing

During implementation stage you actually build your solution. If your project is a software program, this is when you code it.

Keep the needs of your users in mind at all times, as well as your original task statement.

If you are working in a group, it is important to keep everyone on track with their contributions. There are deadlines to be met.

> Implementing involves:
> * building or coding the product.

Evaluating

During the evaluation stage, test your solution and then have others test it.

The users for whom the project was designed are your clients. The solution must meet users' needs, not yours!

Look again at the original task and check that you have fulfilled its requirements.

The solution you have produced should be ethical and accessible to a wide a range of users.

What contribution does it make to our world? Ask if your project is innovative.

Will it be useful and useable in the future? What are suggestions for improvements?

Each time a project ends, you (or your team) should ask these questions:
* What new things did I learn?
* What was the most difficult part?
* What was the most enjoyable part?
* What would I change next time?
* What additional tools do I wish existed?
* What knowledge do I wish I had before starting?
* What could I have done better?

> Evaluating involves:
> * testing the result
> * evaluating against task statement
> * considering improvements.

Knowledge probe: Problems in project management

How the user explained the project to the team

How the project leader understood it

How the project team defined it

How programmers wrote it

How the sales team advertised it

How the project was documented

What was implemented

How the user was charged

How the project team supported it

What the user really wanted

Figure 5.4 Project management problems

Many users and project teams recognise uncomfortable truths in this popular cartoon (Figure 5.4).

1 What is the main point the cartoonist is making?

_____

_____

Knowledge
Probe

2 Write down three things a project team should do to try to avoid some of these issues.

_____

_____

_____

Skill builder: Tools used in project management

This Skill Builder reviews the stages of the design process in project management and can be completed individually or as a fun class activity.

Skill builder

Class activity

Teacher preparation: Use the online PDF to print one copy of the sheet per student or photocopy the next page. Cut up all cards and shuffle them randomly.

Students select exactly 15 cards from an assortment scattered across a desk by the teacher. Pick them up randomly – do not be selective.

Your goal is to collect a complete hand of the 15 different cards, but only by swapping with others. Your final goal is to group the cards under four headings:

- defining
- designing
- implementing
- evaluating.

Individual activity

Your task is to identify the correct stage of the design process for each of the 15 cards and group them under the four headings above.

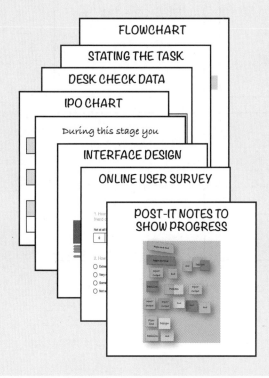

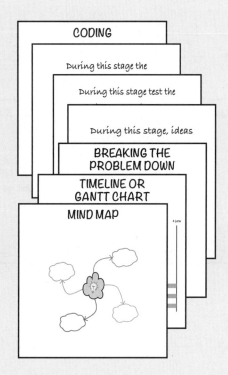

IPO CHART

IPO chart

Processing

Output

INTERFACE DESIGN

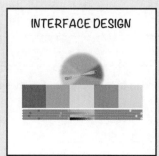

DESK CHECK DATA

Test value	Why this test?	Expected output	Actual output

POST-IT NOTES TO SHOW PROGRESS

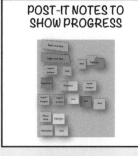

MIND MAP

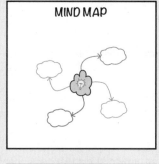

STATING THE TASK

FLOWCHART

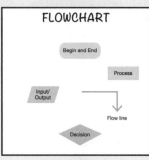

Begin and End

Process

Input/ Output

Flow line

Decision

TIMELINE OR GANTT CHART

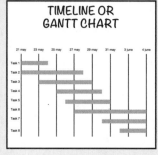

ONLINE USER SURVEY

1. How likely is that you would recommend this software to a friend or family member?

Not at all likely   Extremely likely

| 0 | 1 | 2 | 3 | 4 | 5 | 6 | 7 | 8 | 9 | 10 |

2. How satisfied are you with the reliability of this software?

○ Extremely satisfied
○ Very satisfied
○ Somewhat satisfied
○ Not so satisfied

CODING

```
import random
secret = random.randint(1,100)
print(secret)
flag = True
while flag == True:
    guess = input('Your guess?: ')
    guess = int(guess)
    if guess < secret:
        print('Too low')
    elif guess > secret:
        print('Too high')
    else:
        print('Correct!')
        flag=False
```

BREAKING THE PROBLEM DOWN

During this stage the project is understood, described and broken down

During this stage, ideas are generated and sketched, mock-ups or prototype are developed, algorithms are prepared and user interfaces are planned.

During this stage you produce your digital solution.

During this stage test the solution yourself and then have others test it.

REVIEW

Identify

1 What are the main activities in the defining stage of project management?

_____

_____

2 What are the main activities in the designing stage of project management?

_____

_____

3 What are the main activities in the implementing stage of project management?

_____

_____

4 What are the main activities in the evaluating stage of project management?

_____

_____

Analyse

5 Describe the role of users in project management.

_____

_____

6 Discuss at which stages ethical issues should be considered in project development.

_____

_____

_____

_____

Investigate

7 Agile project management has recently become popular. Research agile project management and summarise how it differs from traditional project management.

_____

_____

_____

_____

_____

Figure 6.1

THE TASK

The number guessing game you started in Chapter 3 is often given as a first programming exercise. It is a great way to begin to learn coding.

Your task now is to improve this guessing game by adding features.

A working version of the earlier game is available on the *Digital Technologies 7 & 8* website. This project may be completed in any general-purpose language. (ActionScript, the Adobe Animate CC coding language, even allows animations to be added in response to guesses.)

This is a guided project. It will help introduce you to the art of programming.

Defining

Here are some ideas for improving our earlier program:
• Generate a new random secret number each time.
• Computer responds with freezing, cold, warm and hot to describe how close users' guesses are (as in hide and seek).
• Count number of guesses the player takes.
• Ask player if they wish to play again.
• Optional: add improvements of your own.

We learnt earlier that programmers define requirements for programs using IPO charts, which have three sections: Input, Processing and Output.

Table 6.1 IPO chart of requirements for improved HiLo game

Input
Integer guess
Processing
Compare secret number to the user's guess and respond with appropriate message depending on how big the gap is
Count guesses
Offer the player a choice to play again
Output
Display appropriate message: 'Freezing', 'Cold', 'Warm', 'Hot', 'Correct!'
Request to play again
Display number of guesses taken

Designing

Adding a play again feature

We add a flag initialised to True. We want the while loop to continue looping until the player guesses correctly. Then we set the flag to False to escape our loop. By placing the main game inside this loop, we can offer a choice of playing again and reset the flag instead to True if our player chooses 'yes'. Note the capital letters for True and False.

Using Python, this is our code so far. Use your earlier version from Chapter 3 or copy and run this program.

```python
import random
secret = random.randint(1,100)
print(secret)
flag = True
while flag == True:
  guess = input('Your guess?: ')
  guess = int(guess)
  if guess < secret:
    print('Too low')
  elif guess > secret:
    print('Too high')
  else:
    print('Correct!')
    flag=False
```

Figure 6.2

We need to capture all the ways a player can say 'yes'. To do this Python has the 'in' keyword, which checks multiple values. This is very handy!

We need to generate a new secret number and ask if the player wants a new game.

So we now add this statement:

```
if play in ['Y','y', 'yes', 'Yes',
'T', 'True']:
```

Copy the code in Figure 6.3 and run it. We have added a temporary print statement to reveal the secret number while we are debugging.

Adding ranges to describe how close guesses are

We now wish the game to include hints such as 'Warm', 'Freezing' and 'Cold' to describe how close the guesses are.

We will be adding features to our earlier game to tell players how close they are to the secret number.

To do this, we need to design ranges for differences between guess and secret number. For example:

- 'Hot' within 5 of the secret number
- 'Warm' within 20 of the secret number
- 'Cold' within 40 of the secret number
- 'Freezing' greater than 40 away from the secret number
- 'Correct!' exactly equal to the secret number.

```
Play again? y
Here we go again
Secret number is 99
Hullo! Guess my number between 1 and 100 20
Freezing
Hullo! Guess my number between 1 and 100 40
Freezing
Hullo! Guess my number between 1 and 100 60
Cold
Hullo! Guess my number between 1 and 100 80
Warm
Hullo! Guess my number between 1 and 100 90
Hot
Hullo! Guess my number between 1 and 100 85
Warm
Hullo! Guess my number between 1 and 100 95
Boiling
Hullo! Guess my number between 1 and 100 98
Boiling
Hullo! Guess my number between 1 and 100 99
Correct! You took 9 guesses
Play again? Y
```

Figure 6.4 This is the output we want to achieve from the improved game.

```
import random                        # import the random module into Python
secret = random.randint(1,100)       # generate a secret random number 1-100
print(secret)                        # print statement added for debugging only
flag = True
while flag == True:
  guess = input('Your guess?: ')
  guess = int(guess)
  if guess > secret:
    print('Too high')
  elif guess < secret:
    print('Too low')
  else:
    print('Correct!')
    secret = random.randint(1,100)        # generate a secret random number 1-100
    print(secret)
    play = input('Would you like to play again? ')
    if play in ['Y','y', 'yes', 'Yes', 'T', 'True']: # lots of the ways to say yes!
      flag = True
    else:
      flag = False
```

Figure 6.3

CHAPTER 6: GUIDED PROJECT: EXTENDED GUESSING GAME

Designing the algorithm

Before looking at the flowchart in Figure 6.5, try drawing one yourself with the improved algorithm.

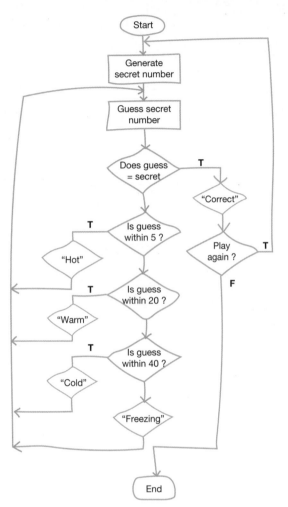

Skill builder

Figure 6.5 Can you explain why these tests would not work if placed in reverse order?

Desk checking logic

Check your flowchart algorithm by testing values shown in the table opposite. Complete all empty spaces. Notice how each possibility is tested and that reasons are given for each test.

In the following, assume your secret value remains 30 for testing purposes.

Absolute value function

We need a way to test how close the player's guess is to the secret number. We can use guess - secret to measure this difference, but it will be a negative answer whenever guess is less than secret.

For example, if the secret is 45 and the guess 30, then:

```
guess - secret
= 30 - 45
= -15
```

Having to handle both positive and negative testing would be messy. Python has a built-in function called abs(), which gives a number's size (magnitude) without the positive or negative sign (also called an absolute value in maths). It is exactly what we need! It looks like this:

```
abs(x)
```

If our secret number is 30, and the player's guess is either 33 or 27 then:

```
abs(guess - secret) = 3
```

for *both* values of guess. We have now created one simple test to avoid the complication of testing both above and below values.

Write out a structured English version of the modified program using the flowchart as your guide and desk check it by using the desk check table (Table 6.2) and assuming the secret number is 30. Structured English makes your coding much easier.

Table 6.2

Test value	Why this test?	Expected output	Actual output
80	Test greater than 40	FREEZING	
70	Test boundary or borderline value	COLD	
65	Test less than 40		
50	Test boundary or borderline value		
40			
35			
33			
30			
Y	At end of game test for "Do you wish to play again?"	Game restarts correctly	
0	Test special case	COLD	
100	Test special case	FREEZING	

Implementing

Code the number guesser program. There will be errors, but you will learn a lot from them. Try to code this on your own and fix any errors. As this is one of your first programming projects using a general-purpose language, we have provided a nearly completed version for you to look at if required (see Figure 6.6). You can find the final version (HiLo4) on the *Digital Technologies 7 & 8* website.

You should add comments to explain new features. When multiple selection is needed, Python uses the keyword elif for 'else if'. Other languages use CASE or SWITCH statements, but the result is the same.

```
import random
secret = random.randint(1,100)
print('Secret number is', secret)
flag = True
count=0
while flag == True:
  guess = input('Hello! Guess my number between 1 and 100 ')
  guess = int(guess)
  count = count + 1
  if guess == secret:
    print('Correct! You took',count,'guesses')
    play=input('Would you like to play again? ')
    if play in ['Y','y', 'yes', 'Yes', 'T', 'True']:
      flag = True
      print('Here we go again')
      # complete code to generate a new random number
      print('Secret number is',secret)
      count = 0
    else:
      flag = False
      print('Bye-bye')
  elif # complete code for guesses within 5
  elif # complete code for guesses within 10
  elif # complete code for guesses within 20
  elif # complete code for guesses within 40
  elif # complete code for guesses outside 40
```
Figure 6.6

Adding a counter

Finally, we have added a counter to record the number of guesses taken each turn and display this when the player guesses correctly.

Evaluating

1 Test the program yourself and have others test it.
2 Identify and correct all errors.
3 Make improvements based on their suggestions.

EXTENSION

Using your knowledge from Chapter 3, rewrite the program using functions. Such an approach makes use of the computational thinking principle of abstraction, which is explained in Chapter 9.

1 Record one thing you learned from this guided project.

_____

_____

_____

_____

_____

_____

2 Can you think of further ideas to improve the game?

_____

_____

_____

_____

_____

_____

_____

_____

_____

_____

_____

_____

_____

07

PROJECT: MULTIPLICATION QUIZ MACHINE

THE TASK

Your task is to create an automatic multiplication generator for a young friend to help them practice times tables. Your program will ask 10 random questions, wait for an answer, report if it is correct and display the final score.

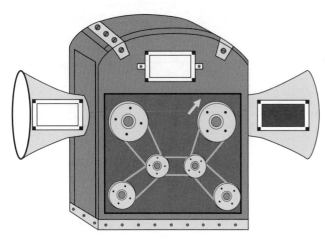

Figure 7.1

Defining

1 Define the problem by using an IPO chart to summarise requirements.
Try this by yourself before looking at our example.

Table 7.1 IPO chart for our guessing game

Input
User selects number of questions
User submits answer to each of multiplication questions

Processing
Program generates two random integers in range 1–12
Program displays questions asking for product of two integers each time
Program checks if each answer equals actual product
Repeat until 10 questions have been asked and answered
Keep score

Output
Display 'True' or 'False' for each question
Display final score

Designing

1 Draw a flowchart on paper to plan your algorithm.
2 When you are satisfied with the logic, write it using structured English. If you need a reminder refer to Chapter 3, page 42.
Remember that indentation is important, as it separates logical blocks.
If there were 10 questions your structured English version might look like this:

```
BEGIN
    set score to 0
    set question count to 0
    WHILE number of questions not
        greater than 10
        generate first number as random
            integer in range 1 to 12
        generate second number as random
            integer in range 1 to 12
        print multiplication question for
            product of first and second
            numbers
        increment question count
        user asked for answer as integer
        IF user answer correct
            print "Correct!"
            increment score
        ELSE:
            print "Incorrect"
    print final score
END
```

Random numbers

3 You will need to generate random numbers. Find out how to do this in your coding language.
In many languages you must import the module that supplies the random number. Check out the way your chosen language handles this.
Chapter 3 introduced the random function.
We will use:

```
random.randint(1,12)
```

Note the dot notation. It shows that randint( ) is a function in the imported random module. Thus, in Python write:

```
first_num=random.randrange(1,12)
second_num=random.randrange(1,12)
```

Incorrect variable types

4 A common source of errors in this type of program is to try to compare variables that are not of the same type. Python expects variables to be the same type as when they were first used. For example, the test below will never be true if the program expects `answer` to be a string and `product` is an integer:

```
if answer==product:
```

Convert an integer into a string by using the function `str ( )` and convert a string to an integer by using `int ( )`.

Implementing

1 Code, debug and run this program in the language of your choice and see if you can get your quiz working.

Evaluating

1 Test your code.
2 Ask others to test it and make suggestions for improvement.

TAKING IT FURTHER

Challenge 1: Modify your code to ask the user if they want to play again and display the total correct as an integer and as a percentage.
Challenge 2: Ask the user for the number of questions they would like.
Challenge 3: After an incorrect answer, print correct answer.
Challenge 4: After an incorrect answer, repeat same question until answer is correct. For an even harder challenge, limit this to a maximum of three attempts.
Challenge 5: Offer addition and subtraction questions (division is very difficult: can you work out why?)
Challenge 6: Offer random mixes of above types.
A suggested solution is provided on the *Digital Technologies 7 & 8* website. See 'quiz_machine.py'.

1 What did you learn from this project?

_____

_____

_____

_____

_____

_____

_____

_____

2 Identify additional features you could include.

_____

_____

_____

_____

_____

_____

_____

_____

_____

_____

08

PROJECT: SIMON SAYS – PROGRAMMING A GAME

THE TASK

Have you ever played a game where you have to remember a sequence that gets longer every time until finally you get it wrong? Your task is to recreate this game!

A popular version of this game is a toy called 'Simon', with four coloured buttons, each making a different sound when pressed. Simon lights up its buttons in a random order, after which the player has to repeat the order by pressing the buttons.

Less guidance has been offered for this project to make it more challenging.

Web probe: Origins

Find out how this game got its name and what words are used in place of 'Simon' in other countries.

_____

_____

_____

_____

Figure 8.1

Defining

1   What variables will you need for this game?
2   What types will each variable need to be?
3   The basis of this game is remembering a sequence of numbers. What data structure can store a sequence of numbers in your computer language?

4   You need to lengthen your sequence by adding a random number each turn. A good way to create this is using the random number function introduced earlier for the secret number in your high–low game (see Chapter 6).

Designing

1   Create a structured English version and then a flowchart to represent the logic for your game and have a class member check these. If they say it is okay, ask your teacher sign off on it.
2   You need a while loop to keep the game repeating as long as the player is remembering correctly.
3   Now we need a new number added each turn. Write out the code in your language to create a random integer from 1–9. In Python it looks like the following (remember to add `import random` as the first line of your code):

```
next=random.randint(1,9)
```

4   You need to have a way of storing the sequence each turn. So far, in your coding you have only needed to store single objects in your variables, such as integers and strings. This time, you need to store a sequence. And you need to be able to add one element to it each turn of the game.

The most common data structure in programming for this is an array.

Array

In computer programming, an array is an ordered sequence of items. Each item has a position or label identified by an index.

The first item is given the index 0, the next one is 1, the next 2, and so on.

For example, consider this array:

```
sequence = [3, 1, 9, 2, 8, 6]
```

Here we see `sequence[0]` = 3 (notice the square brackets) and `sequence[2]` = 9

Your teacher will tell you how to write an array for your chosen class programming language.

In Python, we use the **list** data structure.

It is identical to the above:

```
sequence = [3, 1, 9, 2, 8, 6]
```

Notice again the square brackets.

9780170411813

5 Computer programmers nearly always label the first item in an ordered list, such as an array, the zero position. Do an Internet search to find out why.

_____

_____

_____

_____

6 You need a way to add your new random number each turn. In Python this is easy: add to a list by using the keyword append:

```
sequence.append(next)
```

7 You need to provide a way for the player to enter their guess each time and for this to be stored in another list. Call this new list `playersequence`.
Players need to enter the whole sequence, not just a single number.
The most natural way to ask someone to type a sequence would be to use spaces between each one. Find out how to do this in your language.
In Python, an easy way is:

```
playersequence = [int(x) for x in
    input().split()]
```

Let us examine the separate parts of this code:
`input()` is a function to receive data from the user.
`split()` is a function that looks for spaces and splits up whatever is typed.
`int()` is a function to turn each string into an integer.

8 All you have to do now is check if your two lists `playersequence` and `sequence` are identical.
If they are, print a success message and repeat.
If they are not, print a sorry message and end.

9 Write out your algorithm using structured English. Provided below is a version, if you need it.
Compare this to your flowchart. Even if they are not exactly the same, they can still both be correct. There is usually more than one way to solve a problem in computing!

```
START
create an empty array called sequence
set a flag to true
WHILE flag is true
  create new random integer
  add new term to end of sequence
  print new sequence
  ask player to recall sequence
  IF correct THEN
    set flag to true
    print success message
  ELSE
    set flag to false
    print fail message
  ENDIF
END
```

Implementing

1 Use the structured English version to code in your language.
2 Correct all errors.
3 Often in the implementation stage a designer realises they need to make changes to their design.
After implementing, you probably have realised that players see the whole sequence on the screen displayed after each guess. This makes the game useless for testing memory, but excellent for testing copying!
Can you think of a solution?
A simple solution is to print 20 blank lines onscreen after each new number is displayed. This will scroll the window so the last sequence is hidden.
Notice that this will happen so quickly you need to pause before doing it. Find out how to set a delay in your code.
In Python, import a module called 'time'.
Then use the sleep() function as follows:

```
time.sleep(.75)
```

Challenge 1: Add a message to report the count of the terms each time and modify your code to ask the player if they want to play again.
Challenge 2: Allow the player a choice for the range of integers.
Challenge 3: Keep reporting a highest score while play is in progress.

Evaluating

Test your program yourself and have others test it and suggest improvements.
1 What did you learn from this project?

_____

_____

_____

2 Identify additional features you could include.

_____

_____

_____

REPEATING THE DESIGN CYCLE

It is not often that a design cycle is performed once only. Improvements mean that a programmer will need to work through the cycle again.
Below are some suggested improvements to try.
- Add goals for the number of terms reached and award 'prizes'.
- Allow users up to three attempts.
- Offer a restart option.
- Allow players to choose the number of terms to set a goal.
- Advanced: instead of numbers, create sequences from a set of words.

09

PROJECT: PROGRAMMING YOUR OWN TEXT-BASED ADVENTURE GAME

THE TASK

Your task is to create a text-based adventure game. These games, often known as MUDs, were very popular before computers had graphics abilities that inspired today's graphically intense games.

We begin with a guided example task followed by the main project – creating your own haunted-house adventure!

By completing this project you will learn the skill of thinking computationally.

Web probe: MUDs

Find out about MUDs and explain what this term means.

Skill Builder 1: Building a prototype

Shutterstock.com/breakermaximus

Figure 9.1

The following will guide you through the development of your first version of this game. Your project is to build your own version as part of a group.

Skill builder

Table 9.1 shows the plan of five rooms on the bottom floor of a haunted mansion. You are standing in the foyer and the front door has just slammed shut.

You are only able to enter one of the words: front, back, left or right.

Table 9.1 House plan

	Back door	
Bedroom	Foyer	Lounge
	Front door	

When a player selects a move, an appropriate message is displayed, as follows:

Table 9.2

If they enter here	This happens
Front door	The front door is locked!
Bedroom	You are in the bedroom.
Lounge	You are in the lounge room. The carpet covers broken floorboards and you fall through. The game ends.
Back door	Congratulations, you have escaped via the back door!

9780170411813

Decomposition

Building a large project can be challenging. Breaking a complex problem into parts to allow it to be more easily understood and solved is called **decomposition**. It is the first stage of a skill called **computational thinking**.

Playing this simple game would appear as follows (the program's display is printed blue and the player's responses are black):

```
What is your name? David
Hello, David
You are in the foyer.
There are doorways front, back,
  left and right.
Enter a choice? Front
Congratulations, you have escaped
  via the back door!
Game over
```

In this first version of the game, the player makes only one single move and then quits – not too exciting. Be patient for now.

We use structured English to describe the logic of the game and then use this to write a first coded version. We use decomposition to break down the complexity of the game by thinking about each room separately.

Figure 9.2

1　Draw a flowchart for your game so far.

Below is a structured English version. Notice that it only allows one move and then ends suddenly without explanation.

```
BEGIN
    input name
    print welcome
    tell player they are in foyer
    tell player choice of directions:
    front, back, left, right
    ask player to choose a direction

    IF direction chosen is 'front'
        print message 'Congratulations,
          you have escaped via the back
          door! Game over'
    ELSE IF direction chosen is
      'right'
        print message 'You are in the
          lounge room.'
    ELSE IF direction chosen is 'back'
        print message 'The front door is
          locked!'
    ELSE IF direction chosen is 'left'
        print message 'You are in the
          bedroom.'
    ELSE
        print message 'I don't
          understand that direction'
        print message 'Game over is
          over!'
    END IF
END
```

2　Code, debug and test this first version.

If you need help, a Python version is provided here (Figure 9.3) and on the *Digital Technologies 7 & 8* website.

```python
name = input('What is your name? ')
print('Hello',str(name))
print('You are in the foyer.')
print('There are doorways front, back, left and right.')
direction = input('Enter a choice? ')
if direction == 'front':
    print ('Congratulations, you have escaped via the back door!')
    print ('Game over!')
elif direction == 'right':
    print ('You are in the loungeroom.')
elif direction == 'back':
    print ('The front door is locked!')
elif direction == 'left':
    print ('You are in the bedroom.')
else:
    print ('I don\'t understand the', direction, 'direction.')
    print ('Game over!')
```

Figure 9.3

Skill Builder 2: Adding moves

Skill builder

Now, add two features to make your game more interesting.

- The game must keep going until players enter `quit` or the player enters the lounge room and falls through the broken floor.
- If a player tries to move outside the map or in an empty direction, then the game prints `You can't go` followed by that direction.

Using these new features, here a player incorrectly types an illegal direction – west – instead of left, and then enters the lounge room:

```
What is your name? David
Hello David. You are in the
  foyer. Enter a direction. West
You can't go west.
You are in the foyer. Enter a
  direction. Right
You are in the lounge room. The
  carpet covers broken floorboards
  and you fall through. Game over.
```

1 Draw the flowchart for this new version.

The game loops until the player quits or gets to the back door of the mansion. Note that now you have to handle all possible directions for every room. Previously, you only had to code for the starting room: the foyer.

2 Write the structured English for your game. Take care with indentation.

The earlier structured English you wrote for the foyer will now form part of a chain of `ELSE IF` statements. The others will be much shorter because the other rooms have only one possible move:

```
ELSE IF room is 'bedroom'
    IF direction is 'right'
        set room to 'foyer'
    ELSE
        print message 'You can't go there.'
```

Have a go first, but if you need help, a solution is on the website.

3 Code, debug and test this in your chosen language.

A Python version is on the *Digital Technologies 7 & 8* website.

Skill Builder 3: Data structures

Skill builder

One thing to notice about the last solution is that it requires lots of ugly `IF`, `THEN`, `ELSE` statements, with some even nested inside others!

Your game only has five rooms; imagine if it had 100! There has to be a better way!

You need to make your game *easy to extend*, so more rooms doesn't mean lots more code.

At this stage, you will begin using a *data structure* rather than hard-coding with lots of `IF` statements. Although your game won't have any new features, it will be a lot easier to code.

Notice that once a room is linked to a direction, it leads to a room. So, you could describe your map that way. If you linked these pairs, things will become a whole lot easier.

You have arrived at the second step of computational thinking.

Pattern recognition

The second stage of computational thinking is called **pattern recognition**. This involves finding patterns in data and making sense of data.

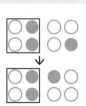

Using pattern recognition

A map of the house can be created using a data structure. Your 'map' will be created by pairing each room exit to a description of the connected room.

You can use a dictionary structure for storing this pattern of paired items. Your chosen language will have some kind of dictionary structure. A dictionary, as the name implies, uses a keyword, known as a *key*, paired to a second word or string called its *value*. When you supply a keyword, the dictionary returns the matching value. Find out how dictionaries are written in your class' language.

In Python, dictionaries are written using curly brackets { }, called braces. The dictionary used for this text book has been named MAP{ }.

The dictionary looks like this:

```
MAP = {
'foyer_front': 'back door',
'foyer_right': 'lounge',
'foyer_back': 'front door',
'foyer_left': 'bedroom',
'bedroom_right': 'foyer',
'front_door_up':'foyer'}
```

The *key* is made up of three parts, which form a string: name of the room + underscore + direction. The paired *value* names the connected room.

If you write MAP['foyer_front'], you get back door

In other words, MAP['foyer_front'] = back door.

Notice the square brackets used in Python to access dictionaries.

Create a second dictionary called DESC{ } and pair room names with their descriptions.

You also need a *list data structure* for items that will end the game. You learnt about lists in the guided project. These are collections of string items separated by commas and enclosed in square brackets.

Call your list FINISH. It looks like this:

```
FINISH = ['back door','lounge']
```

First, you recognised a pattern in what you were doing with rooms in your game. Now, you are representing these patterns using a dictionary data structure. You removed all the detail of room connections and replaced this with a simple model. This is the third stage of computational thinking.

Abstraction

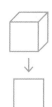

Abstraction is the third stage of computational thinking. Abstraction turns something complex into something simpler by removing detail and reducing it to a general principle or main idea.

You have now turned a messy and complicated game structure (all those IF, THEN, ELSE statements) into something much simpler. Your task is now to redesign your game using a dictionary to model the mansion's rooms.

To see if a direction is legal, all you have to do is ask if the key is in the MAP dictionary using:

```
if key in MAP:
    room = MAP[key]
```

If your key was 'foyer_left', then MAP['foyer_left'] would give the value 'bedroom'.

1 Draw a flowchart for the new algorithm by modelling it on this structured English version:

```
set up MAP dictionary
set up DESCRIPTION dictionary
set up FINISH list of items
ask player name and greet
set start room to 'foyer'
WHILE true
    print description of current
    room using DESC
    IF room is in FINISH dictionary
    THEN
        break
    END IF
```

```
ask player for new direction
IF direction is 'quit'
    break
END IF
create key by joining direction
  and room
IF key is in MAP dictionary THEN
    Legal move and room =
        MAP[key]
ELSE
        print cannot go in this
            direction
END IF
ENDWHILE
message game over
```

By drawing a flowchart and structured English, you have completed the final stage of computational thinking.

Algorithm design

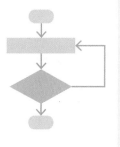

The final stage in computational thinking is called **Algorithm design**. This involves designing a series of ordered steps to solve a problem or achieve some end result, and refining these steps suitable for automation by a computer.

Using the separate computational thinking stages of decomposition, data analysis, abstraction and an appropriate algorithm, you have significantly simplified your code for a five-room house, and made it easy to extend it!

1 Code and run the new game (see Figure 9.4). A final Python version is on the *Digital Technologies 7 & 8* website.

2 Can you think of ways to improve the user experience in this game?

_____

_____

_____

_____

_____

_____

_____

_____

_____

```
#set up dictionaries
MAP = {'foyer_front':'back door',
        'foyer_right':'lounge',
'foyer_back':'front door',
        'foyer_left':'bedroom',
'bedroom_right':'foyer',

'front door_front':'foyer'}
DESC = {'foyer':'You are in the foyer. It is dark and scary. You want to get out! ',
        'back door':'Congratulations, you have escaped via the back door! ',
        'bedroom':'You are in the bedroom. It has been redecorated.',
        'lounge':'You are in the loungeroom. Carpet covers broken boards. You fall through. ',
        'front door':'The front door is locked!'}
#set up list of items that end the game
FINISH = ['back door', 'lounge', 'quit' ]
name = input('What is your name? ')
print ('Hello',name)

test='foyer_front'
print (MAP[test])

#starting location
room = 'foyer'
#loops continuously until a break. Note capital letter in Boolean value True
while True:
  print (DESC[room])
  if room in FINISH:
    break
  direction = input('Enter a direction? Choose from front, back, left, right or quit ')
  key = room + '_' + direction
  if key in MAP:
    room = MAP[key]
  else :
    print ('You can\'t go ' +direction+'. ' )
print ('Game over!')
```

Figure 9.4

Web probe: Computational thinking

1 Search online for the Google video 'Computational thinking'.
2 Summarise how Google uses computational thinking principles.

Weblink

_____

_____

_____

_____

_____

_____

_____

_____

PROJECT: BUILD YOUR OWN ADVENTURE GAME!

By completing the three Skill Builder sections, you will use the following stages of computational thinking to solve a complicated problem:

- decomposition
- pattern recognition
- abstraction
- algorithm design.

Your task now is to complete a project by creating your own game by building on this knowledge.

Defining

1   Clearly define how large your mansion will be.

If using a group approach, form a group of three or four students. You can use a collaborative tool such as Google Docs or Google Sheets so everyone can suggest rooms and descriptions for them.

Designing

1   Map the rooms using a large sheet of paper or whiteboard. You could add a second floor and a basement.
2   When you have finished, draw your map using a computer.

3   (Group only) You might appoint a member to code (implement) special features such as reporting the number of moves players make.
4   (Group only) Decide specialised roles for group members, such as:
- time keepers
- designers
- programmers
- quality controller for code (including spelling)
- quality controller for user experience
- testers
- evaluators
- documenters.

Implementing

1   Code and run your game.

Evaluating

1   Test your game and then have others test it before uploading it for the class to play.
2   Ask: does the final product meet the initial need? Is it innovative and is it adaptable?
3   Play the games developed by others and evaluate them using a collaborative tool using Table 9.3 as your guide.

Table 9.3
(1 is low, 5 is high)

Name of game or group	Level of fun (1–5)	Design skills (1–5)	Level of playing difficulty (1–5)	Rank	Comments

4 What did you learn from this project?

_____

_____

_____

_____

_____

_____

_____

_____

_____

_____

_____

_____

_____

_____

_____

5 Identify additional features you could include.

_____

_____

_____

_____

_____

_____

_____

_____

_____

_____

_____

_____

_____

_____

_____

PROJECT: EMBEDDED SYSTEMS

EMBEDDED SYSTEMS IN THE HOME

If someone asked you how many computers were in your home, you might name a laptop, the family desktop computer and a school laptop or iPad. You might also include smartphones, or your PlayStation or Xbox. However, this would represent only about half the computers in the average house. In most Australian homes there are at least 20 computers, with most of them going unnoticed.

These are called embedded computers or embedded systems. An embedded system is hardware and software that serves a specific single purpose as part of a larger system. Common examples around the home include washing machines, dishwashers, microwaves, DVD players, TVs and network routers.

The Xbox or PlayStation controller has an embedded system using a microcontroller with on-board memory, and the game console has another. Each of these systems has inputs and outputs.

Figure 10.1 Handheld controller from the Xbox One game system

One of the main differences between today's computer games and those of the past is that today's are connected to servers on the Internet. Embedded systems that have a connection to the Internet are referred to as part of the 'Internet of Things' family of devices, or IoT for short.

THE MICROCONTROLLER

In Part 1 of this book you learnt about how the real world is described by analog data, and that most embedded systems use digital data. This chapter will focus your learning on how

The Arduino Uno has 32 KB of flash memory (non-volatile memory), 2 KB of SRAM memory (volatile memory), 1 KB of EEPROM memory (re-writable non-volatile memory) and a processor operating frequency of 16 MHz.

While this seems tiny when compared with today's personal computers, in 1969 the computer on board Neil Armstrong's Apollo 11 spacecraft, which took three men to the moon, had 32 KB of ROM memory (non-volatile memory), 2 KB of RAM (volatile memory) and a processor speed of only 1.024 MHz. So while it may be small, you can do amazing things with it.

Figure 10.2 The Apollo 11 flight computer used in the 1969 moon landing.

Figure 10.3 The Apollo 11 landing crew: Neil Armstrong, Michael Collins and Buzz Aldrin.

an embedded system reads, processes and outputs digital data. In *Digital Technologies 9 & 10* the focus is on how these systems read, process and simulate output of analog data.

This section explores microcontrollers, using the Arduino Uno microcontroller development board (see Figure 10.4).

The Arduino Uno board is one of many boards produced as part of the open-source movement. Open-source hardware and software is developed collaboratively by the community, is not owned by a company and is therefore free for anyone to use.

THE ARDUINO UNO BOARD

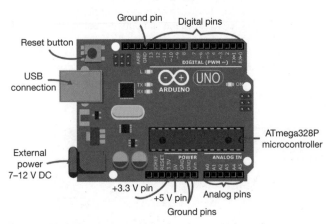

Figure 10.4 The Arduino Uno development board

The Arduino Uno can control a robot, create a light display for a Christmas tree or monitor and control a greenhouse. Its microcontroller chip (ATmega328P) has bootloader

firmware pre-loaded, making it is easy to connect a standard computer for programming.

THE ARDUINO IDE

To program the Arduino Uno board you need a connection to a computer (via USB cable) and software. One of the easiest software applications to use is the Arduino IDE (Integrated Development Environment), which can be downloaded from the Arduino website. A link to this website is provided at the *Digital Technologies 7 & 8* website. The site offers an online tool for writing code, programming your Arduino and sharing code with others.

Weblink

Arduino programs are known as sketches. The very first program that Arduino programmers usually run is the Blink sketch. Blink is also a good program to run to test if your Arduino board is working properly.

For an Arduino sketch to run, there must be at least two things present in the code – the setup function: `void setup( )`, and the loop function: `void loop( )`. The keyword 'void' indicates that this function does not return values.

Within the setup function you place code you want to run once only, and within the loop function you place code you want to run repeatedly. Your first project will help you to understand how these work.

The computer language used for Arduino sketches is called C++ (there is also C language behind the scenes), and the process by which this code is translated into the machine language that the microcontroller can understand is called compiling. C++ is one of many compiled languages.

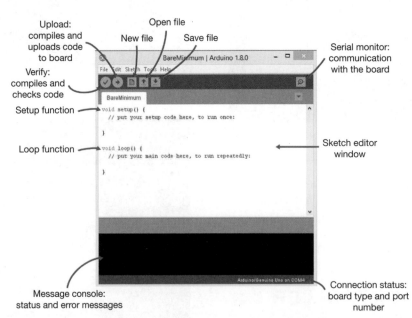

Figure 10.5 A labelled screenshot showing a standard programming window in the Arduino IDE. Within the Sketch Editor window in this screenshot you can see the BareMinimum sketch. When the Arduino IDE is run, it will provide the BareMinimum sketch for you to begin writing code; however, there are many pre-loaded sketches you can access under the File>Examples menu.

PROJECT 1: FIRST SKETCH – BLINK

The first sketch that you will upload to your board is the Blink sketch. The Arduino IDE has a built-in sketch also called Blink; however, the Blink sketch referred to in this project is the one that is included on page 91 and in the Arduino Projects folder for this chapter.

Your teacher will have the following equipment ready for you:
- Arduino Uno board (or equivalent) and USB cable (If you do not have an Arduino Uno, you can complete this project using an online emulator. A link to this has been provided at the *Digital Technologies 7 & 8* website.)
- the Arduino IDE and drivers loaded onto a computer
- project code from the *Digital Technologies 7 & 8* website, downloaded to a folder called Arduino Projects on your computer
- one breadboard
- one LED (any colour will do)
- one resistor between 220 Ω and 330 Ω
- two pin-to-pin breadboard jumper wires (any two colours).

Implementing: Sketch setup

First, construct your circuit as in Figure 10.6 making sure that you have your LED the right way round (see Figure 10.7). LEDs have polarity, which means that there is a positive side and a negative side, so your LED will only light up if you have it connected the right way round. Remember: if you do not have an Arduino board, you can use the link to the online emulator provided on the website.

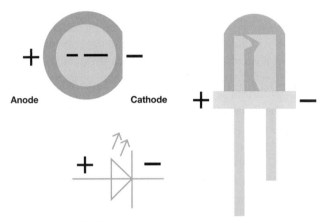

Figure 10.7 LED (light emitting diode) component diagram and schematic diagram. The anode (positive) leg, is usually longer.

Check your resistor is connected in series with your LED. It does not matter if the resistor is connected to the positive or negative side of your LED. Its purpose is to limit the current so the LED does not blow. Think of a resistor as being like a bumpy winding road, which slows cars down as they travel along. Figure 10.8 is the schematic symbol for a resistor.

One of two jumper wires should be connected to the positive side of your circuit and then to pin 3 (digital output pin) on your Arduino board and the other jumper wire to the

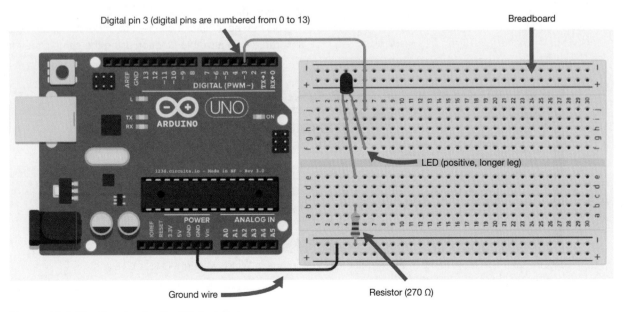

Figure 10.6 Circuit setup for the Blink sketch

Figure 10.8 Schematic diagram of a resistor

negative side of your circuit and GND (ground pin) on your Arduino board.

Once you have your circuit set up and you have your Arduino IDE running on your computer, you can connect your Arduino board to your computer using a USB cable. Check if your Arduino board is properly connected by going to the Tools menu of the Arduino IDE and look at the Ports menu tab to see if you can see a port number (see Figure 10.9).

From the Arduino IDE open a new sketch by clicking on the 'New' tab (or File>New, Ctrl+N).

Type the code below into your new sketch, exactly as it appears, being careful to avoid any syntax errors.

Upload your newly written sketch to your Arduino board by clicking on the 'Upload' button (top left), and observe what happens.

```
/*
*Blink Sketch
*A sketch to blink an LED off and on
*/
int led1=3;//a variable for the LED pin
//the setup function runs once
void setup(){
//initialise led1 pin as an output
  pinMode(led1, OUTPUT);
}
//the loop function runs forever
void loop(){
  digitalWrite(led1, HIGH);
    //turn LED1 on
  delay(1000);
    //wait for a 1000 milliseconds
  digitalWrite(led1, LOW);
    //turn LED1 off
  delay(1000);
    //wait for a 1000 milliseconds
}
```

Testing and evaluating

Did you observe the LED blinking? Did you receive an error code in text console of the Arduino IDE? If your sketch did not work, then you need to correct any bugs in your circuit and code and try to run the code again.

Did you notice at what interval the LED was flashing?

Look at the code. Can you understand how this code made the LED flash? Where is the code that flashes the LED? Is it in the setup function or the loop function? Discuss this with your classmates.

All well-written code has comments to let the human reader understand what each part of the code does. Comments are not part of actual code, and each line of comments must be preceded with two forward slashes, like this //. Identify comments in the Blink sketch code.

Innovating and experimenting

Locate the delay function in the code, which looks like this: **delay(1000)**. There are two instances in this sketch.

Change the values inside the parentheses, then save the code to your Arduino projects folder using a new name. Upload this code to your Arduino board and discuss the results with your classmates.

PROJECT 2: CREATING YOUR OWN BLINK FUNCTION

Take a closer look at the code in the Blink sketch. Did you notice that some words in this code are followed by a set of parentheses, like this ( )? These are known as functions (called methods in some programming languages). If parentheses following a function enclose a value or a variable, this is known as its argument. Arguments are passed into a function, which means that they are used by the function.

This can be a difficult concept to understand, so it will be illustrated with a simple function using the same circuit from

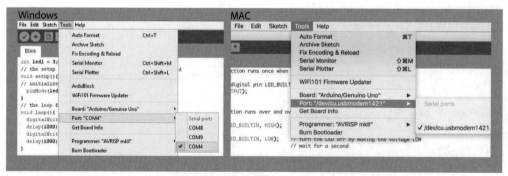

Figure 10.9 The tools menu in the Arduino IDE (left image is Windows, right is Mac). This is where you check for port connection.

your previous sketch. You will add features to allow change to the blinking rate.

1. At the end of the code on a new line after the closing curly brace } of the void loop function, create your new function by giving it a name, such as `blinkRate`. Put the word void in front of it (remember void simply means the function will do something, but not return a value), and include a set of parentheses ( ) after this function name. Place a pair of curly braces { } after this to enclose the doing part of your function.

2. Cut these four lines of code from your sketch

```
digitalWrite(led1, HIGH);
delay(1000);
digitalWrite(led1, LOW);
delay(1000);
```

and paste them enclosed between your function's curly braces.

3. The completed function should look like this:

```
void blinkRate(){
  digitalWrite(led1, HIGH);
  delay(1000);
  digitalWrite(led1, LOW);
  delay(1000);
}
```

Notice that some words are colour coded blue or red. These are special key words used by your language and should not be used for new function or variable names. Notice also that there is a semicolon at the end of each statement within your function. All statements in C++ must end with a semicolon, otherwise the code will return an error.

4. Your program will now run, but it will be easier to use if you add a parameter to this function, which will let you call the function with an argument (value) to control the blink rate. Inside the first pair of parentheses after your function name you declare a variable and define its type. Call this variable rate. Because it will be an integer you will define it by a variable type int. After the delay functions replace the 1000 with a variable rate, like this:

```
void blinkRate(int rate){
  digitalWrite(led1, HIGH);
  delay(rate);
  digitalWrite(led1, LOW);
  delay(rate);
}
```

5. So far you have created a function, but your code will not use it unless you call it inside your loop function. To call your function, include it inside the loop function with an argument inside the parentheses like this:

```
void loop(){
  blinkRate(200);
}
```

6. Finally, because you are good a programmer, you need to comment your code. Type something like this: // a function to blink a LED at a specified rate. The finished code looks like this:

```
int led1 = 3;
//a variable for the LED pin
//the setup function runs once
void setup(){
//initialise led1 pin as an output
  pinMode(led1, OUTPUT);
}
//the loop function runs forever
void loop(){
  blinkRate(200);
    //change the number
    //between the parentheses
    //of the blinkRate function
    //to change the LED's blink rate
}
//a function to blink an LED
//at a specified rate.
void blinkRate(int rate){
  digitalWrite(led1, HIGH);
    //turn LED1 on
  delay(rate);
    //wait for a time period
  digitalWrite(led1, LOW);
    //turn LED1 off
  delay(rate);
    //wait for a time period
}
```

7. Save your code in your Arduino Projects folder using the filename blinkRate, then upload it to your Arduino board by clicking the 'Upload' button in the Arduino IDE. Congratulations! You have just written your first function for your Arduino board. Observe what happens when you run this code and discuss this with your classmates.

Innovating and experimenting

1. Change the value of the argument to your function call. Save the sketch, then upload the code and watch what happens. Example: blinkRate(50); blinkRate(300); blinkRate(2000);

2. Cut the function call (blinkRate(200); from the loop function and paste it in the setup function, then save and upload the code to your Arduino board. What did you observe that was different? Why does it work differently? Discuss this with your classmates.

This project may help you to understand that each function call in a program hides a set of instructions. These instructions lie inside the function definition, which is in another part of the program.

For example: you were able to call your blinkRate function inside the loop function with the simple statement blinkRate(200), because the instructions the blinkRate function needed to execute successfully were placed towards the end of the code inside your blinkRate function definition. In computer programming this is known as abstraction. (Refer to Chapter 9 for an explanation for abstraction.)

PROJECT 3: PUSH BUTTON

Now that you know how a basic Arduino sketch works and how to write some Arduino code, you can try something more challenging.

In this project, you will use a LED (output device) again, but this time you will add a button (input device). After this, you will add further components and create a digital dice.

Your teacher will have the following equipment ready for you to use for this task:

- Arduino Uno board (or equivalent) and USB cable
- the Arduino IDE and drivers loaded onto a computer
- project code from the *Digital Technologies 7 & 8* website, downloaded to a folder called Arduino Projects on your computer
- breadboard
- one LED (any colour will do)
- one resistor between 220 Ω and 330 Ω
- five pin-to-pin breadboard jumper cables (any colours will do)
- one tactile push button (either 4 legs or 2 legs).

Defining: Function and process

You need to define clearly how you want your system to act, and then design it.

The best tools to help you to work this out are the IPO chart and flowchart. In Chapter 5, you learnt how the parts and processes of a system can be represented in visual form with the use of an IPO chart and flowchart.

Table 10.1 IPO chart for a button operated LED system

Input	Process	Output
Button press	Check the state of the button If the button is reading LOW, turn the LED on	+5 volts to LED (use pin 3 for this project)

A flowchart for the loop section of this system would look something like Figure 10.10.

The pushing of the button itself requires a human to perform the action; however, the checking of the button's

status does not require human input. The system will go on checking the status of the button to see if it is HIGH or LOW as long as it has power, regardless of whether or not there is a human controller. This type of system is called a closed loop system, because control is performed by the system itself.

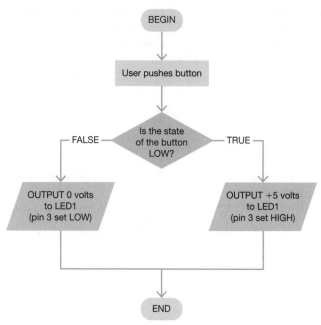

Figure 10.10 Flowchart for a button-operated LED system

Designing: Algorithm

Using this flowchart, you can write structured English to describe your algorithm for this system.

```
LED BUTTON SWITCH
WHILE
   Read button1 status
     IF button1 status is equal to LOW
        Output +5 volts to LED1
        ELSE
          Output 0 volts to LED1
        ENDIF
ENDWHILE
EXIT
```

The IF statement is explained in Chapter 3. In your Arduino code you use an IF statement to check the status of the button.

You need to declare your LED pin and your button pin as variables at the beginning of your code, to tell the program these exist! You also need to initialise their state as either input or output.

The entire code for your system written with Arduino language looks like this:

```
int led1 = 3; // the LED pin
int button1 = 2; // the button pin
bool buttonState = HIGH;
//variable to hold the button's state
```

```
void setup(){
  pinMode(led1, OUTPUT);
  //initialise led1 pin as an output
  pinMode(button1, INPUT_PULLUP);
  //initialise button1 as input pullup
}
void loop() {
buttonState = digitalRead (button1);
//read the state of button1
//if the button state
//is reading low (pressed)
//then set led1 to high,
//else, set led1 to low
if(buttonState == LOW){
  digitalWrite(led1, HIGH);
}
else {
  digitalWrite(led1, LOW);
}
}
```

Notice the delay function is not used in this sketch because the LED is only on when the button is being pressed.

Also, notice that button 1 is initialised as INPUT_PULLUP. This is a special type of input that uses an internal resistor in the Arduino board to ensure that when your button is not pressed it is reading HIGH. If you did not use this type of input for your button, your button status would float between HIGH and LOW whenever the button was not being pressed, resulting in your LED randomly flashing on and off.

Implementing: Sketch setup

You need to set up your circuit as shown in Figure 10.11.

You have one LED attached to ground (GND) via a 270 Ω resistor on its negative side, and connected to pin 3 on the Arduino board via a jumper wire on its positive side. Notice that you connected the ground (GND) on your Arduino to the negative (−) rail at the bottom of your breadboard using a black jumper wire,

and then connected this to the negative (−) rail at the top of your breadboard using a second black jumper wire. This is to give you more ground connections, which you will need for your next project.

You have connected your button on one side directly to ground via a jumper wire, and to pin 2 via a jumper wire on the other side.

Test and evaluate

1 Set up your circuit as shown in Figure 10.11.
2 From your Arduino Projects folder, open and upload the pushButton sketch to your Arduino board.
3 Push the button in your circuit and observe what happens.
4 Debug your circuit if the LED does not light up when you push the button.
5 Discuss with your classmates.

PROJECT 4: CREATING A DIGITAL DICE

Turning a light on and off is obviously very useful in certain situations, but in the case of your project, how could it be more useful? Most real-world projects are designed to meet a need.

If you think about your project in the context of computer games, you might have an answer.

Generating random numbers is very useful in computer games. In fact, without them, games would play the same way every time (you were able to see how the random function worked in Chapter 3).

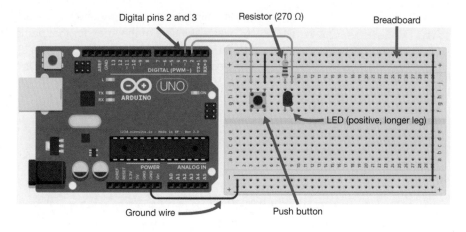

Figure 10.11 The setup for the pushButton sketch

One of the simplest and most useful random number generators is a six-sided dice. Six-sided dice have been used in game playing since ancient times.

A dice is a great choice for your project because you can easily adapt your existing circuit.

For this extension your teacher will supply (also use the materials previously listed):

- seven LEDs (any colours)
- seven resistors between 220 Ω and 330 Ω
- 11 pin-to-pin breadboard jumper cables (any colours).

Designing: The Digital_ Dice code

You now have seven LEDs in this sketch, which require seven digital pins to be declared inside the code.

You could declare them all one by one like this:

```
int led1 = 3;
int led2 = 4;
int led3 = 5;
int led4 = 6;
int led5 = 7;
int led6 = 8;
int led7 = 9;
```

This would work, but you can imagine how messy your code would look if you needed 1000 LEDs in a project! You can use a data structure called an array to help you declare all variables at once:

```
int led_pins[]= {3,4,5,6,7,8,9};
```

All your LED pin numbers are enclosed between a pair of curly brackets with a comma separating each.

In computer programming, counting always begins from 0, so if you wanted to count out five items you would do it like this: 0,1,2,3,4.

The variables inside your led_pins array are counted as shown in Table 10.2.

Arrays make it easy to perform tasks that contain a number of repeated steps. In your code, you use a FOR loop to set the pin mode for each of your LED pins, like this:

```
for (int thisPin = 0; thisPin < 7;
   thisPin ++){
   pinMode(led_pins[thisPin], OUTPUT);
}
```

This FOR loop starts at 0 and goes up to 6 in steps of one for each turn of the loop, and for each turn, one of the pins within your array is initialised as an output, starting with the first (pin3) and finishing with the last (pin9). See details earlier in Chapter 3.

You can use a FOR loop to access your array any time you need to perform repetitive tasks in your program, like turning all of the LEDs off:

```
for (int thisPin = 0; thisPin < 7;
   thisPin ++){
   digitalWrite(led_pins[thisPin], LOW);
}
```

Defining: The dice pattern

A traditional dice layout looks like Figure 10.12.

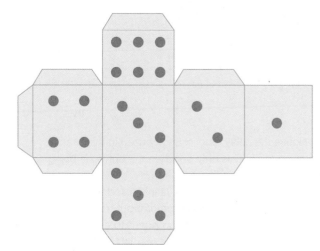

Figure 10.12 A standard six-sided dice pattern

To obtain the correct dice pattern when your LEDs turn on, you need the correct LEDs set to HIGH within each IF statement.

The IF statement used inside your code looks like this (below) when the number 3 is 'rolled':

```
if (ran == 3){
   digitalWrite(led_pins[2], HIGH);
   digitalWrite(led_pins[3], HIGH);
   digitalWrite(led_pins[4], HIGH);
   delay(pause);
}
```

The number inside the square brackets after each led_pins variable name relates to the position of the element inside of the array for that particular LED variable. So in this example, you have led_pins[2], led_pins[3], led_pins[4], which correspond to pins LEDs 3, 4 and 5 (pins 5, 6 and 7).

Table 10.2 Numbering configuration for the led_pins array

led_pins	0	1	2	3	4	5	6
	Pin3 (LED1)	Pin4 (LED2)	Pin5 (LED3)	Pin6 (LED4)	Pin7 (LED5)	Pin8 (LED6)	Pin9 (LED7)

Designing: Skeleton code

Type the following code exactly as a new program using your Arduino IDE.

Incomplete sections are indicated and you will be completing these in the following section.

Save your program as Digital_Dice_Project_(followed by your initials).

```
int led_pins[] = {3,4,5,6,7,8,9};
int button1 = 2;
int buttonState;
int ran;
int pause = 1000;

void setup() {
for (int thisPin = 0; thisPin < 7;
  thisPin++) {
  pinMode(led_pins[thisPin], OUTPUT);
}
  pinMode(button1, INPUT_PULLUP);
  randomSeed(analogRead(A0));
}
void loop() {
  buttonState = digitalRead(button1);
  if (buttonState == LOW){
    ran = random(1, 7);
    if (ran == 1){
      digitalWrite(led_pins[3], HIGH);
      delay(pause);
    }
    if (ran == 2){
//MISSSING CODE
    }
  if (ran == 3){
  digitalWrite(led_pins[2], HIGH);
  digitalWrite(led_pins[3], HIGH);
  digitalWrite(led_pins[4], HIGH);
  delay(pause);
  }
  if (ran == 4){
  //MISSSING CODE
  }
  if (ran == 5){
  //MISSING CODE
  }
  if (ran == 6){
  //MISSSING CODE
  }
}

  for (int thisPin = 0; thisPin < 7;
    thisPin++) {
  digitalWrite(led_pins[thisPin], LOW);
}
}
}
```

This code is more complicated than other code you have used so far. Don't worry if it looks a little confusing at first.

Designing: Array task – fill in the blanks

Table 10.3 on the next page shows what the pattern should look like for each number of the dice. The first three numbers have been done for you, but it is your task to fill in the sequence for numbers 4 to 6.

Now complete the missing parts of your code from the last section.

Save your completed version!

Build and test a prototype

Now build a prototype (see Infobit below) dice emulator as shown in Figure 10.13. If you do not have a physical Arduino board, you can use the online emulator. A link has been provided at the *Digital Technologies 7 & 8* website.

Weblink

Upload your completed code to this prototype and test it.

> **INFOBIT: PROTOTYPE**
>
> A prototype is a limited working version of a final product, often used to test a design, especially with users.

Implementing: Sketch setup

If you have an Arduino board, it is now time to build a physical version of the dice emulator. Set up your circuit as shown in Figure 10.13. This can be a tricky circuit, so take extra care to ensure that you have your LEDs the right way round. Ensure each LED is connected to GND via a resistor on its negative side, and connected to the correct digital pin via a jumper cable on its positive side.

The LEDs are set out as close as possible to a traditional dice pattern, because it is not possible to align them perfectly on the breadboard.

> **INFOBIT**
>
> There are some devices available that have components pre-attached, so that you do not need to mess around with the wiring. Some of these devices are the Wiltronics ARD2-INNOV8-Shield, the MAAS ThinkerShield and the MakersBox FunShield.

Table 10.3 LED configuration to make a traditional dice pattern

LED1		LED2
LED3	LED4	LED5
LED6		LED7

digitalWrite(led_pins[3], HIGH);

LED1		LED2
LED3	LED4	LED5
LED6		LED7

digitalWrite(led_pins[2], HIGH);
digitalWrite(led_pins[4], HIGH);

LED1		LED2
LED3	LED4	LED5
LED6		LED7

digitalWrite(led_pins[2], HIGH);
digitalWrite(led_pins[3], HIGH);
digitalWrite(led_pins[4], HIGH);

LED1		LED2
LED3	LED4	LED5
LED6		LED7

digitalWrite(   );
digitalWrite(   );
digitalWrite(   );
digitalWrite(   );

LED1		LED2
LED3	LED4	LED5
LED6		LED7

digitalWrite(   );
digitalWrite(   );
digitalWrite(   );
digitalWrite(   );
digitalWrite(   );

LED1		LED2
LED3	LED4	LED5
LED6		LED7

digitalWrite(   );
digitalWrite(   );
digitalWrite(   );
digitalWrite(   );
digitalWrite(   );
digitalWrite(   );

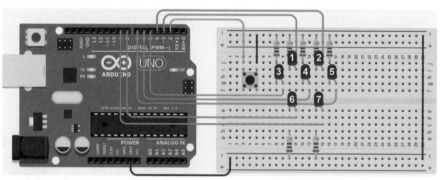

Figure 10.13 Setup for the Digital_Dice sketch

Test and evaluate

1 Set up your circuit the same as the circuit in Figure 10.13.
2 Connect your Arduino board and create your Digital_Dice_Project sketch in a new file, and save it to your Arduino Projects folder.
3 Upload your completed sketch to your Arduino board, then push the button in your circuit and observe what happens.
4 Debug your circuit if LEDs do not light up in the correct sequence with each push of the button.
5 Discuss the results, and how you overcame any issues, with your classmates.
6 To view the completed code example open the Digital_Dice_Complete file in your Arduino Projects folder.

Questions

1 How many input devices does this system have? How many output devices does this system have? What are they?

_____

_____

_____

_____

_____

_____

_____

_____

_____

_____

_____

_____

9780170411813

2 Identify and list in order the control structures and data structures in this code.

_____

_____

_____

_____

_____

_____

_____

_____

_____

_____

_____

3 How many conditional (IF) statement blocks are there? Could you replace an IF with an ELSE statement? Adjust your code to try this.

_____

_____

_____

_____

_____

_____

_____

_____

_____

_____

_____

_____

_____

FINAL PROJECT CHALLENGES

If you look at the loop function in your completed Digital_Dice sketch, you will notice that there is a lot of code.

This is not such a problem here; however, if you needed to add additional processes this would mean more lines of code, leading to a messy sketch.

Programmers make their programs elegant. This means that they try to write programs using as few instructions as possible in order to use minimum memory. Many programmers view writing elegant code as an art form.

You may have realised from the Arduino sketches that you have studied so far that there is more than one way to write a program. The challenge is to find the most elegant way.

For your final task in this section you will be left with four challenges, in increasing order of difficulty

1 Using your knowledge of functions, eliminate as many lines as possible within the loop section of your Digital_Dice sketch. This can be as easy as cutting a number of lines from within the loop function and pasting them inside your function. The difficulty is in knowing which code to move and how to structure it. Ask 'does it need an argument?' Remember to call your function within the loop, and be sure to structure your function like this:

```
void functionName(){
    //place your function code here
}
```

Could the code be further simplified with the use additional/different data and control structures?

2 When a user holds down the button in your version of the program, the dice keeps rolling. Modify the code so that only one result shows on the dice and stays on until the button is pressed again.

3 Your Digital_Dice sketch is fine for a person who has good eyesight, but what about people with impaired vision? Design a system with audio output (such as a piezo buzzer), which signals the number rolled. Use the Digital_Dice sketch as a base for your new design.

Searching 'Arduino Tone Melody' will lead to a tutorial to help with this task.

4 Modify your code so that your program flashes a rapid sequence of random results until finally settling on one outcome – just like a real dice!

Example solutions for these challenges can be found in your Arduino Projects folder.

GUIDED PROJECT: USING SPREADSHEETS

absolute addressing Cell references in a formula using absolute addressing remain the same as you copy from one cell to another

cell The intersection of a row and a column in a spreadsheet, identified using a letter and a number, e.g. A3

column A vertical set of data items in a spreadsheet, identified using letters

relative addressing Cell references in a formula using relative addressing change as you copy it from one cell to another

row A horizontal set of data items in a spreadsheet, identified using numbers

spreadsheet An application using rows, columns and formulas to organise and store data requiring calculation

The first **spreadsheet** ever invented, VisiCalc (short for 'visible calculator'), was the software that popularised the first Apple computers. For a year the Apple II was the only computer with a spreadsheet program (Figure 11.1).

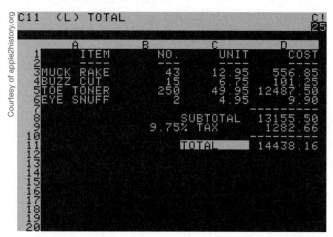

Figure 11.1 VisiCalc, the first spreadsheet used by Apple computers from 1979

Like many world-changing inventions, it began with a very simple idea: a student, Dan Bricklin, was watching his lecturer use a chalkboard to summarise business calculations. As the lecturer changed a value in the table he would then erase all the connected values one by one and rewrite them. Dan realised software could automate this. His 'magic sheet of paper' was a completely new way for people to use a computer, and it was created less than 40 years ago!

WHAT IS A SPREADSHEET?

A spreadsheet is a program that uses rows and columns to organise, store and make calculations from data.

A **cell** is created where a row and a **column** intersect. Cells are named using the letter of the column and the number of the **row**. In Figure 11.2, Patrick Jennings' name is in cell A11 and his Total Bonus is in cell F11.

What are spreadsheets used for?

In business, spreadsheets can be used to present reports, make financial predictions, and create charts and graphs. A teacher can use a spreadsheet to track student marks.

Spreadsheets can simulate or model real-world situations, such as how much money is owed in each year of a loan or model climate change.

Popular spreadsheet applications are Microsoft Excel, Google Sheets and Apple Numbers. Examples will cover both Microsoft Excel and Google Sheets.

9780170411813

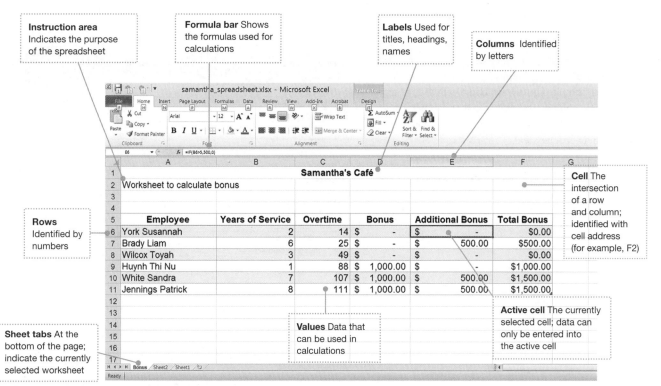

Formula bar Shows
the formulas used for
calculations

Labels Used for
titles, headings,
names

Columns Identified
by letters

Rows
Identified by
numbers

Cell The
intersection
of a row
and column;
identified with
cell address
(for example, F2)

Active cell The currently
selected cell; data can
only be entered into
the active cell

Values Data that
can be used in
calculations

Sheet tabs At the
bottom of the page;
indicate the currently
selected worksheet

Figure 11.2 The basic elements of a modern spreadsheet

Activity probe: Entering data and formulas

Imagine you have just successfully built your first drone from parts bought online. Friends ask if you can build them one just like yours. You decide to use a spreadsheet to track costs and profits.

1 The items you require to build your drone are listed in Figure 11.3. Set up a new spreadsheet and copy these details into it.

2 Set this data type as Currency.

After entering all values, highlight column C and choose one of the following:

- If using Excel: Format > Cells or on the ribbon under the Home tab choose Number then Currency.
- If using Google Sheets: Format > Number > Currency.

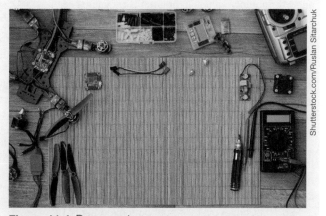

Figure 11.4 Drone parts

Drone item	Quantity per drone	Each
Transmitter and receiver	1	$54.00
Frame	1	$18.00
Flight controller	1	$99.00
Power distribution board	1	$2.20
ESCs (electronic speed control)	4	$9.50
Motors	4	$15.00
Prop adapters	4	$2.00
Battery	1	$24.00
Charger	1	$23.00
Adapter for battery	1	$3.80
Power supply	1	$10.00
Props	1	$3.00
Tall nylon spacers	4	$1.25
Short nylon spacers	4	$1.10
3.5mm bullet connectors	2	$2.10

Figure 11.3

Figure 11.5 An assembled drone

Activity probe: Writing your own formulas

Spreadsheets help keep numbers organised, but they really show off their power in calculations. For this, you need formulas.

To use a formula, you always begin with the '=' sign. This tells the spreadsheet software that you want a calculation to be done, and that what follows is not to be treated as ordinary text.

Addition

= B2 + C2 means add together the values in the two cells.

Subtraction

= B2 − C2 means subtract the value in C2 from the value in B2.

Division

= B2 / C2 means divide the value in B2 by the value in C2. Keyboards use '/' because the ÷ sign can be mistaken for a plus sign.

Multiplication

=B2 * C2 means multiply together the values in the two cells. Keyboards use an asterisk symbol (*) because the × sign can be mistaken for the letter X.

You can use the spreadsheet to calculate the total cost of a number of items. For example, you need four motors, one for each propeller. This means you need to multiply values in column B by values in column C along each row by writing a formula in a new column D.

To do this, enter the formula = B2*C2 in cell D2 and press Enter/Return. The result in D2 will show as $54.00 (Figure 11.6). You could write a similar formula in every cell from D2 down to D16, but this would be boring, easy to make mistakes and take a long time.

One of the 'magic' things about spreadsheets is that they can recognise patterns and apply them over a range of cells. You can now use this built-in ability, called Fill Down.

To do this, hover over the right bottom corner of D2 where a crosshair will appear, then drag this crosshair down from D2 to D16.

If you do this then all the totals will be calculated automatically and appear in column D (Figure 11.7).

	A	B	C	D
1	Drone items	Quantity	Each	Total
2	Transmitter and receiver	1	$54.00	$54.00
3	Frame	1	$18.00	
4	Flight controller	1	$99.00	
5	Power distribution board	1	$2.20	
6	ESCs (electronic speed control)	4	$9.50	
7	Motors	4	$15.00	
8	Prop adapters	4	$2.00	
9	Battery	1	$24.00	
10	Charger	1	$23.00	
11	Adapter for any battery	1	$3.80	
12	Power supply	1	$10.00	
13	Props (pack of 4)	1	$3.00	
14	Tall nylon spacers	4	$1.25	
15	Short nylon spacers	4	$1.10	
16	3.5mm bullet connectors	2	$2.10	

Figure 11.6

	A	B	C	D
1	Drone items	Quantity	Each	Total
2	Transmitter and receiver	1	$54.00	$54.00
3	Frame	1	$18.00	$18.00
4	Flight controller	1	$99.00	$99.00
5	Power distribution board	1	$2.20	$2.20
6	ESCs (electronic speed control)	4	$9.50	$38.00
7	Motors	4	$15.00	$60.00
8	Prop adapters	4	$2.00	$8.00
9	Battery	1	$24.00	$24.00
10	Charger	1	$23.00	$23.00
11	Adapter for any battery	1	$3.80	$3.80
12	Power supply	1	$10.00	$10.00
13	Props (pack of 4)	1	$3.00	$3.00
14	Tall nylon spacers	4	$1.25	$5.00
15	Short nylon spacers	4	$1.10	$4.40
16	3.5mm bullet connectors	2	$2.10	$4.20

Figure 11.7

Check formulas in each of the cells of column D. The first is

=B2*C2

then

=B3*C3
=B4*C4

and so on. The spreadsheet has guessed the pattern in each row. Spreadsheets not only guess patterns in formulas but can do the same with numbers, and even words!

9780170411813

Select a column in a new spreadsheet and use two rows to enter the values 1 and 2. Highlight both of these values. Hover over the right bottom corner of the lower cell where a crosshair appears, and drag downwards (Figure 11.8). The spreadsheet guesses the pattern. This is also a great way to automatically number lots of rows. Magic!

Try the same things using 2 and 4 (Figure 11.9).

Then try out some word patterns (Figure 11.10).

Figure 11.8

In Excel there is also a Fill Down menu item you can use under the Home tab, but in this case you must first highlight the range of cells you wish to Fill.

The Fill method also fills patterns across the columns of spreadsheets.

G
2
4
6
8
10
12
14
16
18
20
22

G
drone a
drone b
drone c
drone a
drone b
drone c
drone a
drone b
drone c
drone a
drone b
drone c

Figure 11.9   Figure 11.10

Activity probe: Using built-in formulas

You now want to find the total of all values in column D.

You could write this in column D17:

= D2 + D3 + D4 + D5 + D6 + D7 + D8 + D9 + D10 + D11 + D12 + D13 + D14 + D15 + D16

Fortunately, spreadsheets have formulas built in. The one you need for this activity is for sum, SUM( ), which adds the values within cell ranges.

All formulas begin with '=' and use parentheses for the values they need for their calculations. Here, you use a colon to indicate the range of cells to sum.

Enter = SUM(D2:D16) into cell D17.

Press Enter/Return and you will see this total calculated for you (see Figures 11.11 and 11.12).

	A	B	C	D
1	**Drone items**	**Quantity**	**Each**	**Total**
2	Transmitter and receiver	1	$54.00	$54.00
3	Frame	1	$18.00	$18.00
4	Flight controller	1	$99.00	$99.00
5	Power distribution board	1	$2.20	$2.20
6	ESCs (electronic speed control)	4	$9.50	$38.00
7	Motors	4	$15.00	$60.00
8	Prop adapters	4	$2.00	$8.00
9	Battery	1	$24.00	$24.00
10	Charger	1	$23.00	$23.00
11	Adapter for any battery	1	$3.80	$3.80
12	Power supply	1	$10.00	$10.00
13	Props (pack of 4)	1	$3.00	$3.00
14	Tall nylon spacers	4	$1.25	$5.00
15	Short nylon spacers	4	$1.10	$4.40
16	3.5mm bullet connectors	2	$2.10	$4.20
17	TOTAL PARTS			=SUM(D2:D16)

Figure 11.11

A summary of useful formulas appears at the end of this section.

TOTAL PARTS	$356.60

Figure 11.12

Improving your spreadsheet: Adding features and formatting

Building the drone takes around three hours. You decide labour is worth $12 per hour.

Add rows 18 and 19 with appropriate calculations entered in D18 and D19 and show total cost. See Figure 11.13.

17	TOTAL PARTS			$356.60
18	LABOUR @ $12 p.h.		3	$12.00	$36.00
19	TOTAL COST			$392.60

Figure 11.13

You decide you need to build in some profit! Set this at 15 per cent.

Add 0.15 to cell C20 and format this to Percent using the Format menu item.

Enter an appropriate calculation in cell D21 to give a final total retail price for the drone. See Figure 11.14.

18	LABOUR @ $12 p.h.	3	$12.00	$36.00
19	TOTAL COST			$392.60
20	Profit		15.00%	$58.89
21	Final retail price for customer			$451.49

Figure 11.14

Looking good!

The examples above have been made easier to read by the use of colours. Note that words are centred, headings are in large bold text, colours are pastels, and the final total is highlighted. Use the formatting tools in your spreadsheet to design your own easy-to-read layout.

Activity probe: Representing data using charts

Charts allow you to more easily turn data into information. There are many different types of charts or graphs available and they each have their own strengths and weaknesses.

Pie chart

A pie chart could be used to show the breakdown of costs for the parts needed for the drone.

You can see clearly that the flight controller, transmitter/receiver and motors make up around half the total cost of materials.

Try creating this pie chart yourself using your existing data.

You need to select only the data in columns A and D, which contain the names of the items and the total costs. By holding down the Ctrl/Cmd key you can highlight only data in columns A and D.

To insert a chart, select Insert from your spreadsheet menu. Select the pie chart style.

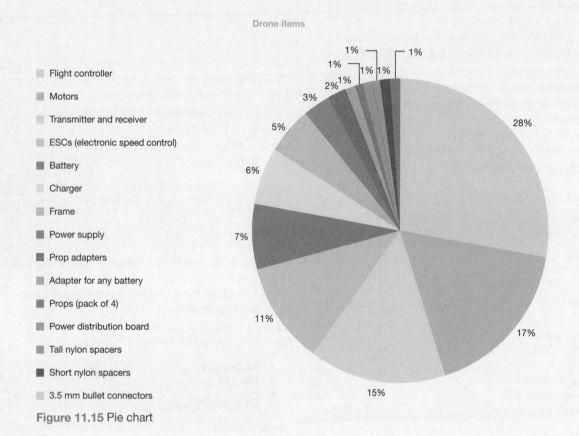

Figure 11.15 Pie chart

9780170411813

Column chart

It is possible to create different worksheets within the same spreadsheet in both Excel and Google Sheets.

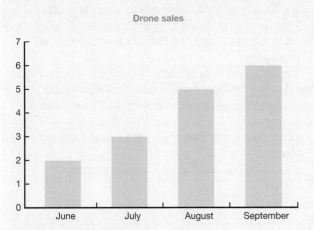

Figure 11.16 Column chart

Create a new worksheet by clicking on the '+' sign at the base of the window. It will automatically be named Sheet2.

Below is a worksheet of sales for June to September.

Copy the following new data by entering it into Sheet2 of your spreadsheet.

Use the menu to create a column chart by highlighting this data and inserting the correct chart.

	A	B	C	D	E
1		June	July	August	September
2	Drone sales	2	3	5	6

Figure 11.17

A column chart clearly shows a trend upwards, where a pie chart would not.

Line chart

Sales are so successful that your drone builder has decided to form a business called 'HomeGrownDrones'. The company will offer two models, the Standard and Pro.

Sales figures are entered into row 3 of the spreadsheet and a line chart is chosen.

A line chart will show clearly the increasing popularity of the Pro drone over the Standard model.

Create this line chart by entering the following data into a spreadsheet (Figure 11.18).

	A	B	C	D	E
1	**Sales figures**	**October**	**November**	**December**	**January**
2	Standard drone	5	4	3	3
3	Pro drone	2	4	5	6

Figure 11.18

A line chart allows you to examine trends between these two products.

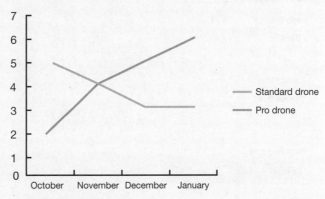

Figure 11.19 Line chart

Selection of data

If you want to graph only the Standard drone from the data in Figure 11.18, you would select only rows 1 and 2 and choose a chart type. Try doing this.

If you want to chart only the Pro drone, you would select only rows 1 and 3. Select rows 1 and 3 only by holding down the Ctrl/Cmd key.

Activity probe: Conditional formatting

Spreadsheets allow you to set rules for when cells change colour, known as conditional formatting.

First select the row showing the Drone totals.

Suppose that you cannot make more than eight drones a month. You want to be warned when this happens. In both Excel and Google Sheets the conditional formatting tool appears under Format in the menu bar. In Excel it also appears on the ribbon under the Home tab.

In Excel, choose Conditional formatting > Manage rules, click the '+' symbol and select Classic style from the drop down menu.

Choose Format only cells that contain and greater than and finally the value 8 (Figure 11.20).

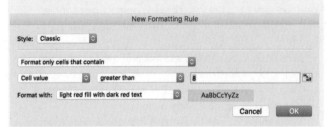

Figure 11.20

In Google Sheets, choices appear in a panel at the right edge of the spreadsheet (Figure 11.21).

You will see that drone totals for January now have a red background and bold text because their total exceeds 8 (Figure 11.22).

Figure 11.21

	A	B	C	D	E
1	Sales figures	October	November	December	January
2	Standard drone	5	4	3	3
3	Pro drone	2	4	5	6
4	Drone totals	7	8	8	9

Figure 11.22

Activity probe: Linking data from other worksheets

Sheet2 contains your sales figures but suppose you want to graph profits.

On Sheet1 you need to add data for your Pro drone.

They are identical to the Standard drone except you need to add three items and drop two items: Motors and Prop adapters.

To create a new list of parts for the Pro drone, copy and paste all the Standard drone data into an empty space on that spreadsheet *after* the existing used rows. Leave a gap between.

Insert three empty rows at the top by using the Insert function.

Enter additional data for the Pro drone as follows.

Table 11.1

Electronic speed control improved version	1	14.33
Motors better bearings less vibration	4	17.95
High performance props	4	5.2

All existing formulas automatically adjust values for new rows.

Make sure formulas are added for the three new items to give totals.

Delete the old row for Motors (you have just added higher quality ones!).

Delete the row for Prop adapters (no longer required).

Check carefully all formulas are correct (Figure 11.23).

Notice that you make greater profit on the Pro drone.

	Pro drone	Quantity	Each	Total
24				
25	Electronic speed control improved ver:	1	14.33	$14.33
26	Motors better bearings less vibration	4	17.95	$71.80
27	High performance props	4	5.2	$20.80
28	Transmitter and receiver	1	$54.00	$54.00
29	Frame	1	$18.00	$18.00
30	Flight controller	1	$99.00	$99.00
31	Power distribution board	1	$2.20	$2.20
32	ESCs (electronic speed control)	4	$9.50	$38.00
33	Battery	1	$24.00	$24.00
34	Charger	1	$23.00	$23.00
35	Adapter for any battery	1	$3.80	$3.80
36	Power supply	1	$10.00	$10.00
37	Props (pack of 4)	1	$3.00	$3.00
38	Tall nylon spacers	4	$1.25	$5.00
39	Short nylon spacers	4	$1.10	$4.40
40	3.5mm bullet connectors	2	$2.10	$4.20
41	TOTAL PARTS			$395.53
42	LABOUR @ $12 p.h.	3.5	$12.00	$42.00
43	TOTAL COST			$437.53
44	Profit		15.00%	$65.63
45	Final retail price for customer			$503.16

Figure 11.23

9780170411813

Moving ranges of cells

To move cells, place the cursor at the top right corner of a highlighted range of cells where the icon changes to a hand. Drag highlighted cells to the new position.

Referencing other sheets within a spreadsheet

To find each month's earnings, you need to multiply the number of each drone by the profit it makes and add them together.

You need to get the profit data from Sheet1 and multiply these by the data for the numbers sold, which only appears in Sheet2.

In mathematical language:

Your earnings for each month

= sales standard drone × profit standard drone + sales pro drone × profit pro drone

In Sheet2 in cell A4 write a label 'Earnings'.

The method used by most spreadsheets to refer to other worksheets in the same spreadsheet is by their name, followed by '!' and the cell reference from that worksheet, like this: Sheet1!D20

Using this method, in B4 enter:

=Sheet1!D20*B2 + Sheet1!D44*B3

and press Enter/Return (Figure 24)

	A	B	C	D	E
1	Sales figures	October	November	December	January
2	Standard drone	5	4	3	3
3	Pro drone	2	4	5	6
4	Earnings	$425.71			

*fx =Sheet1!D20*B2 + Sheet1!D44*B3*

Figure 11.24

See if your total is correct.

To save typing, Fill right by dragging B4 by its small crosshair to the right (Figure 11.25).

	A	B	C	D	E
1	Sales figures	October	November	December	January
2	Standard drone	5	4	3	3
3	Pro drone	2	4	5	6
4	Earnings	$425.71	0	0	0

Figure 11.25

Something is wrong! Where did all those 0s come from? We solve this problem next.

Activity probe: Relative and absolute addressing

If you check the formulas, you will see formulas in cells C4 to E4 are:

=Sheet1!E20*C2 + Sheet1!E44*C3
=Sheet1!F20*D2 + Sheet1!F44*D3
=Sheet1!G20*E2 + Sheet1!G44*E3

All the orange and blue cell references are incorrect.

The way a spreadsheet guesses patterns is by using **relative addressing**. As formulas move down rows or across columns cell references change to match. You do not want Sheet1 references to change, as they refer to the unchanging cells D20 and D44.

There is a way to lock cell references when you Fill Down or Fill Across. This is called **absolute addressing**. Do it by adding a '$' sign in front of the cell reference you want unchanged.

Correct your first entry in cell B4 to:

=Sheet1!$D$20*B2 + Sheet1!$D$44*B3

Fill right again and it should now show correct profits (Figure 11.26).

	A	B	C	D	E
1	Sales figures	October	November	December	January
2	Standard drone	5	4	3	3
3	Pro drone	2	4	5	6
4	Earnings	$425.71	$498.08	$504.82	$570.45

Figure 11.26

Check each formula and see how Sheet1 cell references stay fixed.

Which chart type would be suitable for displaying Earnings here in Sheet2?

If you want to change a chart's axis scale or appearance, just click on the axis and these choices will be offered, both in Excel and Google Sheets.

SPREADSHEET FORMULAS SUMMARY

It is useful to look at the large number of formulas built in to your spreadsheet program. They are collected under categories such as:

- maths
- statistics
- counting
- text
- financial
- date and time.

In Excel, under the Formulas tab an icon Reference, and in Google Sheets the icon Σ, will allow you to browse all functions.

Useful spreadsheet formulas

Formula	Example	Explanation
SUM	=SUM(A1:A5)	Returns the sum of values in the range A2:A7
IF	=IF(A1>50, "big", "small")	Returns the word 'big' if the value in A1 is greater than 50, and returns 'small' otherwise.
COUNT	=COUNT(A1:A10)	Returns the number of cells in the range A2:A7 that contain numbers
COUNTIF	=COUNTIF(A1:A10,">5")	Returns number of cells in range A2:A7 that contain a value greater than 5
MEAN or AVERAGE	=AVERAGE(A2:A7)	Returns the average of values in the range A2:A7
MEDIAN	=MEDIAN(A2:A7)	Returns the value in the middle position of the range A2:A7 when all the values are sorted
MODE	=MODE(A2:A7)	Returns the value appearing most often in the range A2:A7
RANDOM	=RAND( )	Returns a random number between 0 and 1
	=RANDBETWEEN(1,10)	Returns a random integer in the range 1 to 10 inclusive
VLOOKUP	=VLOOKUP (A1, F2:G26, 2)	In this example, VLOOKUP searches in cells in column F for the value closest to A1 and returns the corresponding value from column G. The last integer indicates the column from which to retrieve the value

9780170411813

This project starts with a story.

A king was asked by a suitor for his daughter's hand in marriage. He answered that he would only give permission if the man brought him a chessboard filled with rice according to the following pattern:

One single grain on the first square of the board, two on the next square, four grains on the next, and so on – doubling the number of grains for each square until the last one was filled.

The man attempted the task but failed.

He bought many sacks of rice but finally decided that the task was impossible.

In this project you will use spreadsheet skills you learned in Chapter 11.

Figure 12.1 The King's chessboard

THE TASK

Your task in this project is to design and build a spreadsheet to find out if the suitor's task is possible. Imagine that the chessboard is a huge one so that grains will fit inside each square, no matter how many there are!

Your spreadsheet should:
- show the number of grains on each square of the chessboard
- show the weight in metric tonnes on each square of the chessboard
- show the total grains on the chessboard
- show the total weight of the grains on the chessboard
- automatically have cells change colour and print a message on rows where the annual world rice harvest is exceeded
- calculate the cost of the rice in Australian dollars for each square and for the total.

Information you will use:
- Each grain weighs 0.025 grams.
- There are 1000 grams in 1 kilogram and there are 1000 kilograms in a tonne.

Web probe: Global rice production

Conduct an Internet search to find how many tonnes of rice were produced globally last year. The easiest way to do this to use data from the Food and Agricultural Organisation (FAO) of the United Nations.

Defining

1   Before you get started, make a prediction. Do you think there are enough grains of rice in the world for this task?

_____

2   Use this grid to represent a chessboard and complete as many numbers for the grains on each square as you can manage.

1	2	4	8	16	32	64	128
256							

3   How many grains of rice would be required on the last square?

_____

4   You know the weight of each grain. Write out a rule for converting the number of grains to tonnes.

_____

_____

5   Using the Web probe above, record the total tonnage of rice produced globally last year.

_____

6   Compare results from more than one source. Comment on how reliable you believe each source for this data is. Choose a reliable answer.

_____

_____

_____

_____

_____

_____

_____

_____

Designing

1   Decide how your spreadsheet will be organised.
2   Set up columns you will need and headings for these columns.
3   Fill the chessboard square numbers 1 to 64 down the rows of a spreadsheet by using a formula and Fill Down.
4   Fill the grain counts 1, 2, 4, 8, 16 and so on, down through the 64 rows of the spreadsheet.
5   What is the largest integer you can enter into a cell of your spreadsheet?

_____

6   Try entering a number with more than 15 digits then press Enter/Return. What happens?

_____

_____

7   Use the Internet to find what is the largest positive number that can be used in Excel and what is the highest precision allowed for any number.
    Advanced: What is the difference between the size and the precision of a number? What is the highest precision allowed for any number in Excel?

_____

_____

_____

8   Design user-friendly features you would like for your spreadsheet: conditional formatting (e.g. make the numbers red) to show when/if the grains on a particular square exceed the total global rice crop, print message if annual world rice crop is exceeded.
9   Make sure to include the total of grains of all the squares at the end.
10 Add a formula to calculate approximately the total value in Australian dollars (AUD) of all grains on the board. You will find this in United States dollars (USD) but you need to convert this using your formula into Australian dollars.

Implementing

1   Build the spreadsheet and include all features outlined in the task description (Figure 12.2).
2   Make changes as needed.
3   Test your results are 'sensible'.
4   Compare your results to those of other students.

Evaluating

1   Does the suitor get to marry the princess?

_____

2   Does this result surprise you?

_____

Chessboard square	Number of grains	Weight in metric tonnes	Value in AUD
19	262144	0	$4.39
20	524288	0	$8.78
21	1048576	0	$17.56
22	2097152	0	$35.13
23	4194304	0	$70.25
24	8388608	0	$140.51
25	16777216	0	$281.02
26	33554432	1	$562.04
27	67108864	2	$1,124.07
28	134217728	3	$2,248.15
29	268435456	7	$4.496.29

Figure 12.2 Calculations for squares 19 to 29 of the chessboard spreadsheet. Is your answer correct?

3 How many times more than the total world rice crop would be required for the last square alone?

_____

_____

_____

4 How could your spreadsheet be improved?

_____

_____

_____

_____

_____

_____

_____

_____

EXTENSION

1 What would be the total value of the chessboard and its rice based on the current world price per tonne of rice?

_____

_____

_____

2 How does the limitation on number size and number precision of a spreadsheet affect these results?

_____

_____

_____

_____

_____

_____

_____

_____

_____

3 A common use for a spreadsheet is to handle money. Such dollar amounts would often exceed 15 digits. Are you surprised that Excel cannot handle these? Use the Internet to research this limitation and summarise what you discover.

_____

_____

_____

_____

_____

_____

_____

_____

_____

_____

4 What did you learn by completing this project?

_____

_____

_____

_____

_____

_____

_____

_____

_____

_____

5 Identify additional features you could include that would make your spreadsheet more user-friendly.

_____

_____

_____

_____

_____

_____

_____

_____

13 PROJECT: BUILD YOUR OWN INTERACTIVE TEMPERATURE CONVERTER

THE TASK

Your task is in two parts, which together form this project.

Part 1: In the first part, you will use a special scroll bar/slider control built into Excel to interactively change cell values (most people do not know this feature exists!) to simulate a thermometer (see Figure 13.2).

In Figure 13.2, all the grid lines of the spreadsheet have been turned off.

Teachers: note that Part 1 is a guided project.

Part 2: In the second part, you will repeat the design cycle with different data and design your own interactive spreadsheet to process it.

This project cannot be completed using Google Sheets because it does not have built-in controls such as sliders.

Figure 13.1 Celsius and Fahrenheit scales on a mercury thermometer

PART 1: GUIDED THERMOMETER PROJECT

Defining

1   Research which major countries use Fahrenheit and which use Celsius for measuring temperatures.
2   In cell B3 write the label Celsius.
    In cell B5 write the label Fahrenheit.

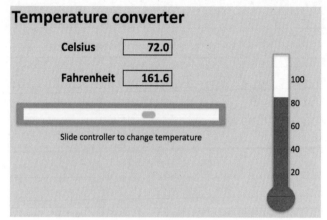

Figure 13.2 The final interactive temperature converter

3   Format cell C3 and C5 with a border around them (as in Figure 13.2).
4   The formula for converting Celsius to Fahrenheit is
    $$F = \frac{9}{5}C + 32$$
    Enter this as a spreadsheet formula into cell C5 by using a reference to cell C3 as your input Celsius value.
    Try out these values to check if it works:
    0°C = 32°F, 100°C = 212°F, 76°C = 168.8°F

Designing

1   Use the drawing tools in Excel to draw a thermometer. Combine a rectangle with a circle. Make the Fill for the circle red. Make the rectangle fill white. Do not draw a slider.

Implementing

1   Animate the thermometer by adding the formula =$C$3 to the column of cells inside the narrow rectangle you drew for the thermometer by using Fill Down.
2   Explain why this cell reference uses '$' signs for absolute referencing.

_____

_____

_____

_____

_____

9780170411813

3 Add the slider. Excel does not show the Developer tab unless it is turned on. Turn on this Developer tab in the Excel Preferences > Ribbon > Developer and select the scroll bar (slider in some versions of Excel) control listed under Form Controls.

4 Right-click on the scroll bar control and insert a link to cell $C$3 via Format Control. Set up your slider control using the settings shown in Figure 13.5. Test out your slider.

5 Turn the text in the cells that are inside the thermometer white and set the background fill to white.

6 Use conditional formatting separately on each cell in the thermometer to trigger a change to bright red fill for the cell and an identical bright red for the font, whenever the value in that cell exceeds set cut-off values.

Note that you need to choose Style of Conditional Formatting to be Classic and 'Use a formula to determine which cells to format' from the dropdown choices given. Your rules will look like Figure 13.3.

7 Make grid lines invisible. Try to achieve the effect shown in Figure 13.2.

Evaluating

1 Check the accuracy of your spreadsheet converter.
2 Ask users to test it.
3 Make improvements.

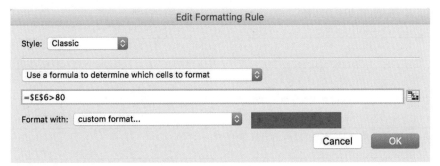

Figure 13.3 Setting Conditional Formatting

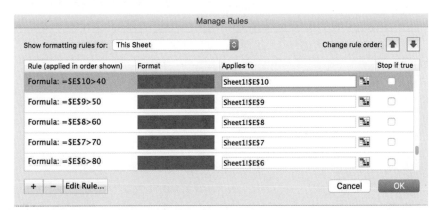

Figure 13.4 Conditional Formatting rules

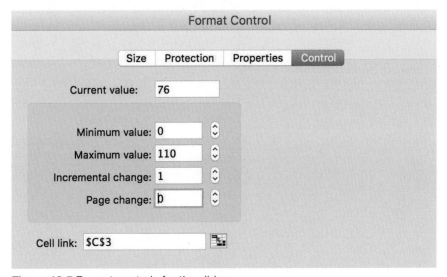

Figure 13.5 Format controls for the slider

PART 2: INDIVIDUAL PROJECT

In this Part, you are on your own.

Find two sets of numerical data that commonly require conversion. Some possibilities include:

- centimetres to inches
- kilometres to miles
- currency conversions
- kilometres per hour to miles per hour
- advanced: currency conversion using live daily rate (Hint: research how to use live web queries in Excel). Work through identical stages of the design cycle as in Part 1 to design and build your own digital solution.

1   What did you learn by completing this project?

_____

_____

_____

_____

_____

_____

_____

2   Identify additional features you could include.

_____

_____

_____

_____

_____

_____

_____

_____

_____

_____

_____

_____

_____

9780170411813

PROJECT: ROLL THE DICE

THE TASK

Your task in this project is to:
- design and build a spreadsheet to automate two dice being tossed 100 times and to find the most common total
- extend it to design and build a spreadsheet to automate the tossing of two coins.

Shutterstock.com/Andrei Shumskiy

Figure 14.1 Your spreadsheet will be a lot faster than tossing these 100 times!

Link to the Arduino project

Project 4 in Chapter 10 teaches you how to build an electronic dice using LEDs. These two projects are great to complete together!

Defining

1 Guess what total appears most often when two dice are thrown and the dots are added together. Write it here.

_____

If you have access to dice, toss them multiple times and write down the totals. Use Table 14.1 to record your results.

2 Preparing for this project is an important step. Carefully research and respond to the following questions:

  a Could you get 1 as a total? What are all the possible totals that can occur?

  _____

  _____

  b What built-in spreadsheet formula could be used to simulate the toss of a dice?

  _____

  _____

Table 14.1 Experimental results using actual dice.

Dice 1	Dice 2	Total

  c How will you obtain a total of the results on two dice?

  _____

  _____

  _____

  d Which spreadsheet software will you use?

  _____

  e What is the most number of rows allowed in your spreadsheet software? Look it up on the Internet.

  _____

f Find how to force your spreadsheet software to recalculate and so create new random numbers as if tossing dice again. This is possible in both Excel and Google Sheets, but the approaches are different in each.

_____

_____

_____

_____

_____

g Your goal is to find the most common total. Look up the meanings of the following statistical terms and decide which one describes what you need here:
- mean
- median
- mode.

  Find the spreadsheet formula you need for this for your spreadsheet.

_____

_____

3 How could you create a pie chart to display the total occurrences for each result from 2 to 12 for 100 tosses?

_____

_____

_____

_____

_____

_____

4 What other features could you add? Some suggestions are:
- Count the occurrences of possible totals each time.
- Display the most common total each time.
- Use conditional formatting.
- If using Excel, add a button with a macro using Excel Developer tools to recalculate the spreadsheet each time it is pressed. Excel does not show the Developer tab unless it is turned on. Turn on this Developer tab in the Excel Preferences > Ribbon > Developer and select the button control listed under Form Controls. Draw the button on your spreadsheet. Right-click the button and choose Assign Macro. Type this macro for the button:

```
Sub Button1_Click()
Sheet1.Calculate
End Sub
```

Designing

1 Design a layout for your spreadsheet. Ask other students for their comments.

2 What columns and rows will you need? What formulas will be used?

  Hints:
- Use the built-in RANDBETWEEN ( ) formula to simulate the toss of a dice.
- Use built-in COUNTIF ( ) formula to obtain a count of a particular value in a range of cells.

3 How many rows will you use?

4 Will you include any charts?

Implementing

Now it's time to build your spreadsheet! Refer to your design decisions and add all features. Test your result against the task requirements and have others test it.

Adding an animated die

1 It is possible to set up Excel to create a simulation of the image of an actual dice being tossed.

  The secret is to notice that dice have a grid of nine dots. Set up a 3 × 3 grid of cells to imitate this, using Excel (you need to narrow the column and rows).

2 Set up cell E1 to simulate the throw of a dice using =RANDBETWEEN(1,6).

3 You need to find a symbol for a dot. There are various ways to get a suitable black dot. You could set the cell's font to Wingdings and use the formula =CHAR(108) in the cell.

4 Your challenge now is to enter appropriate =IF ( ) formulas in each of the nine cells in the grid, which will cause them to print dots when they should, based on the number in cell E1 (Figure 14.2).

  For example, cell A2 only needs to show a dot when a 6 is thrown. Using CHAR(108) to print the dot if 6 occurs and to print nothing otherwise, the formula will be =IF(E1=6,CHAR(108)," ")

  If you want an IF statement to check when a cell contains one of many things, you can use an OR like this:

```
=IF(OR(test 1, test 2, test 3...),
  result if true, result if false)
```

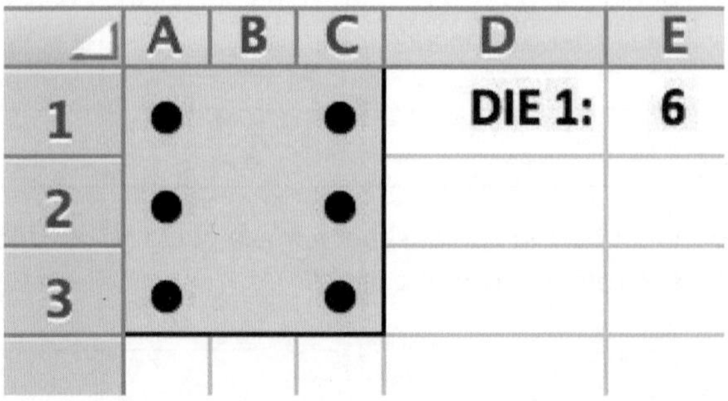

Figure 14.2 Creating dots on a dice using a formula

5 Create a second dice and print a message whenever both dice match!

6 You can re-toss the dice by recalculating the Excel spreadsheets. Use the Recalculate All button on the ribbon or the F9 key (Mac and Windows) or add a button using a control on the Developer ribbon with a macro rule assigned (Figure 14.3).

Evaluating

1 Did the result surprise you? Can you explain it?

_____

_____

_____

_____

_____

2 Does your spreadsheet experiment mean this result will always be true?

_____

_____

_____

_____

_____

3 Did other students find the same result?

_____

_____

_____

4 Could the limit on the number of rows allowed in a spreadsheet affect your results?

_____

_____

_____

_____

5 How could your spreadsheet be improved?

_____

_____

_____

_____

_____

_____

_____

_____

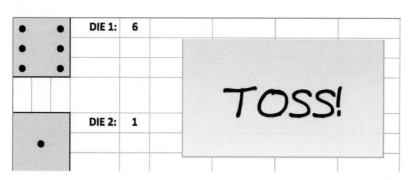

Figure 14.3 The final result with a button and macro for tossing the dice

EXTENSION 1: COIN TOSS

The task

Use what you have learnt to create another spreadsheet to simulate the tossing of two coins 100 times and write the total heads and tails.

1   How will you randomly generate either a head or a tail?
    Hint: One way is to use the RAND ( ) function, which will generate a random decimal value between 0 and 1. Then use the formula:

    =IF(B3>0.5, "Heads", "Tails")

2   What did you learn by completing this project?

_____

_____

_____

_____

_____

_____

_____

3   Identify additional features you could include.

_____

_____

_____

_____

_____

_____

_____

EXTENSION 2: CODING

The task

Now a challenge! Try using a general-purpose programming language to achieve the same outcome as this spreadsheet.

9780170411813

15

GUIDED PROJECT: IMAGE EDITING

THE TASK

Your task in this guided project is to master the main features of an image editing application, such as Photoshop.

Professional-level image editing software offers an amazing variety of ways to manipulate an image. Photoshop is the most widely used and popular image-editing software application. It is so popular that 'photoshopping' has entered everyday language as a verb to describe this type of photo alteration.

This chapter will use Photoshop for all examples, but other image-editing software, such as GIMP, is available free online. This guided project will introduce you to Photoshop but is not intended to be a complete course. Apart from class lessons, there are many online tutorials and courses you can use to explore its powerful possibilities.

A useful sequence to follow when starting out with image editing is as follows:
• become familiar with the interface
• learn how selection works
• learn about layers
• learn to use colour, gradient effects and text.

Open Photoshop and as each feature is explained, cross it off the list above.

You will follow this sequence in the Skill builder activities in this chapter.

Photoshop interface

The Photoshop interface is divided into main parts: Menu bar, Toolbox, Options, Palettes and Document window.

The Menu bar runs across the top of the screen and contains menu options for common tasks.

Options Bar/Control panel
This panel changes depending on what tool has been selected. For example, if you're using the Brush tool, you'll be able to change the brush size and hardness, brush tip, opacity, flow and more.

Tools panel
The tools are very important in Photoshop. You use these for editing your images.

Colour picker tool
Here, you can select the colours for various tools, such as the Brush tool, the Gradient tool, and many others. Current foreground and background colours are shown.

Panels
Here the main panels are displayed. The first group are the Colour and Swatches panels, the second group contains Adjustments and Styles, and the third contains Layers, Channels, and Paths. To work with a panel, activate it by clicking its tab. Many more are available.

Document window
This is where your image editing takes place. More than one image can be opened at once. Tabs appear above each one.

Layers panel
This is the most important panel in Photoshop. Artwork can be separated into layers, like stacked transparencies. You can turn each layer on and off by clicking the eye icon. The active layer is highlighted.

Figure 15.1 The Photoshop interface

The Toolbox contains tools you use to create and modify images, grouped into categories. Options along the top of the Photoshop window change according to the tool chosen.

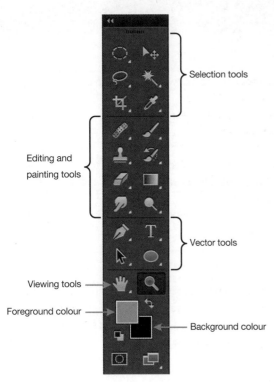

Figure 15.2 The Toolbox

Palettes offer more functions. The two you will use most often are Colour and Layers. Palettes can be grouped, moved separately or closed.

Selection tools

Holding Shift while using a selection tool will add to a selection, whereas holding opt/alt will subtract.

After a selection is made, use the Move tool to cut the selection and move it. Hold opt/alt to duplicate it. Any selection can be freely transformed by the Edit > Free Transform.

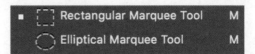

Figure 15.3 Selection shapes

Rectangular Marquee: Selects rectangular areas.
Elliptical Marquee: Selects ellipses or circles if Shift is held. Holding opt/alt with mouse button down will centre the selection.

Figure 15.4 Magic Wand

Magic Wand: Click to select connected areas of similar colour. Adjust tolerance from Options bar. Hold down Shift key to add to selection.

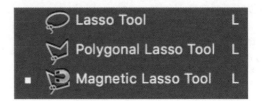

Figure 15.5 Selection tools

Lasso and Polygonal Lasso tools: Lasso Tool is for freehand selections.
Magnetic Lasso: Click on the starting point before dragging along the outside edge of an object.

Table 15.1 summarises the various tools in image-editing software.

Table 15.1 Common image editing tools

Category	Tools and effects	Description of effect
Brush tools	Pencil	Draws a hard-edged line of any thickness
	Brush	Draws an anti-aliased line that blends with the background
	Airbrush	Applies a fine spray of colour like an airbrush
Edit tools	Smudge	Smears part of the image
	Blur/sharpen	Reduces/increases colour contrast
	Dodge/burn	Lightens/darkens part of the image
	Sponge	Reduces or increases saturation and contrast
Selecting	Marquee	Selects regular-shaped parts of an image for manipulation
	Lasso	Selects irregular-shaped parts of an image for manipulation
	Magic wand	Selects contiguous (connected) regions of pixels with the same colour (tolerance can be adjusted)
Masking	Mask	Selects an outline expressed as a greyscale image – selected areas appear white, deselected areas appear black, feathered edges are shades of grey
	Quick mask	Turns currently unselected area into a mask that can then be modified

9780170411813

Category	Tools and effects	Description of effect
Filling	Paint bucket	'Pours' the foreground colour or pattern into an area bounded by pixels of one colour – a similar concept to 'colouring inside the lines'
	Fill	'Pours' the foreground colour or pattern into a pre-selected area
	Gradient	Fills a selected area with a multi-colour gradient
Duplicating and erasing	Rubber/clone stamp	Copies the pixels from a specified area of the image to a new area
	Eraser	Reverts the selected area to the bare background colour
Undo	History	Reverts to a previous step in your work – the palette displays the steps taken in the order they occur
Text effects	Type	Enters and edits text, and applies embossing and drop shadows

Skill builder: Learning selection tools

In this task, you can create either:
- a zany fruit face composed of bits of fruit and vegetables
- a steampunk face made up of springs and gizmo from mechanical parts.

1

Figure 15.6 Selection tools put to work

Select which image you will create. Either find images of fruit and vegetables or mechanical bits and pieces using images from the Internet or other sources (a suggestion: search for watch parts). Choose an image for the head. Choose images that would be suitable for the parts of the face.

For example, the mechanical face image shown here is a jumble of watch parts where contrast was lowered using Image > Adjustments > Brightness/Contrast followed by a vector mask.

2 Create a new document using Photoshop. Drag all images into the one window to form separate layers. Select a suitable image to be the head. Make the head the bottom layer.

3 Select suitable images for the eyes. Use the Elliptical Marquee to select the shape, then duplicate it and position them on the face.

4 Select an image for the nose. Resize if necessary. Use the Magnetic Lasso to select it, duplicate it and drag it onto the face.

5 Select an image for the ears. Use the Magnetic Lasso to separate parts of a larger object, duplicate it and position it on the face.

6 Select an image for the mouth. Use the Magic Wand to select all pixels of the same colour, duplicate and drag this onto the face.

7 Crop the final result and, if you wish, add a drop shadow as shown in the mechanical face image.

Skill builder: Working with layers

Every Photoshop image contains one or more layers. New layers are transparent until artwork is added. A checkerboard background indicates the transparent areas.

The Layers palette can be used to hide, view, reposition, delete, rename and merge layers.

In Figure 15.7 there are two layers: the background of the soccer field and the soccer ball in Layer 2.

Think of layers as being like transparent sheets on top of each other. An eye icon on a layer indicates that the layer is visible and the active layer is highlighted.

Adding artwork in new layers from other image files

1 Go to the *Digital Technologies 7 & 8* website and download and open the files soccer_field.psd and soccer_ball_poster.psd and separate into two floating windows by dragging the tab for the soccer ball poster file.

Figure 15.7

2 Use your knowledge of selection, from the last section, to select around the soccer ball using the Elliptical Marque selection tool.

3 Choose the Move tool and drag the selected soccer ball onto the other window.

The file that has been dragged appears on a new layer (Layer 1). Double click on the new layer and rename it 'soccer ball'.

Hiding and showing a layer

1 In the Layers palette, click in the space on the extreme left of the soccer ball layer name to turn the visibility of the soccer ball off and on. An eye icon on the left of a layer indicates the layer is visible. A blank space indicates the layer is hidden.

2 Create another layer to include a small prepared soccer poster.

3 Make all layers visible and open the 5VS5_poster file.

4 Select it all and drag it onto the existing image of the soccer field. A new layer will be created. Name it 'poster'. (Figure 15.8)

You now have three layers as shown: poster, soccer_ball and background (Figure 15.8).

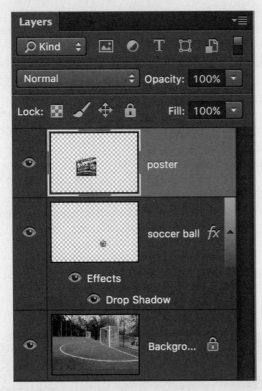

Figure 15.8 Three layers: poster, soccer_ball and background

1 Drag the poster over the edge of soccer ball. You will see it covers it. Layers highest up in the palette are in front.

2 In the Layers palette, drag the poster layer below the soccer_ball layer. The soccer ball now appears above the poster (Figure 15.9).

Changing layer opacity

Reducing the opacity allows images on other layers to show through.

1 Make the soccer_ball layer active.

Figure 15.9 Selecting the poster layer

2 Click on the Opacity in the Layers palette and drag the slider to make the ball see-through. Return to 100% opacity. Try this on the poster layer too.

Changing layer blending mode

The blending mode controls how pixels in an image are affected by a painting or editing tool.

1 Click the Mode Menu dropdown to the left of Opacity in the Layers palette.

2 Experiment with selections from the list. Detailed descriptions of each mode are available online.

Linking layers

Linking two or more layers together enables them to be moved or altered simultaneously, maintaining their alignments.

1 Select the two layers at once. Click the chain link icon at the base of the Layer palette. A link icon will appear in the layers (Figure 15.10).

Figure 15.10 Linking layers

Adding new layers

To add a new layer, click the turned-up-edge page icon at the base of the Layers palette. This will create a transparent layer with no artwork. It will appear in the Layers palette above the active layer.

Adding gradient effects

A gradient is a gradual transition between one or more colours.

1 Add a new transparent layer above the layer to which the gradient effect is to be applied.

2 Choose the Linear Gradient tool in the Toolbox to select the tool and its Options palette (appearing at top).

3 Select the type of gradient from the Gradient picker dropdown box in the Gradient Options palette.

4 Change the colours by double-clicking on the lower colour stops. Change the opacity using the stops.

5 Make sure the new empty layer is active, and drag the Gradient tool across the image in the required direction. If necessary, change the Opacity of the gradient layer.

Adding text

Text is to be automatically placed in a new layer, identified by a large letter T.

1 Select the Type tool.

2 Click on the image where the text is to be placed. Type Options will appear at the top in the Options panel.

3 Select text colour, font, style and size.

Add special effects to text

These effects can include shadow, glow, bevel and emboss, among others.

1 Ensure the text layer is active.

2 Click Layer > Layer style and choose the effect required.

3 Try adding a drop shadow. Make adjustments to the settings.

Final touches

You will need the following files: soccer_field and soccer_ball_poster.

1 Recreate this image using the skills you have acquired.

2 Tick off the following features as you achieve them:

   ☐ Create new file with soccer_field as the background.

   ☐ Selection tools to extract soccer ball from soccer_ball_poster and create new layer with soccer ball.

   ☐ Add soccer_ball_poster as new a layer and apply a soft drop shadow effect to this layer.

   ☐ Add a glow around the soccer ball.

   ☐ Position the soccer ball on top of the poster.

   ☐ Add a blue gradient layer at the base.

   ☐ Add text with drop shadow over the gradient.

3 What did you learn by completing this project?

_____

_____

_____

_____

_____

_____

_____

_____

4 Identify additional features you could include.

_____

_____

_____

_____

_____

_____

_____

_____

_____

_____

_____

Figure 15.11 Refining your skills

16

PROJECT: A MOSAIC MURAL FOR THE CLASSROOM

THE TASK

Your task is to create a large-format wall mural of a single A1 sized image made up of eight separate panels, each sized to A4. You will be assigned eight Photoshop activities from a lucky dip, forming separate parts of the larger image.

By the end of the project, you will have explored the special effects possible in Photoshop and created a wall hanging from a mosaic of images.

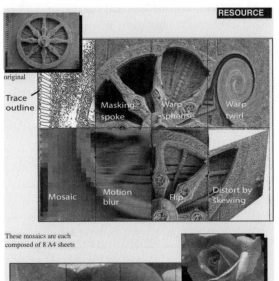
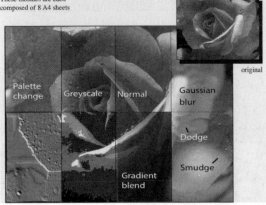

Figure 16.1 An example mural using eight panels

Defining

Your teacher will create a lucky dip of choices by printing and cutting up the PDF provided online at the *Digital Technologies 7 & 8* website (reproduced below).

Mural task cards

Experiment with various palettes, replacing some colours with others for a pleasing result	Use an airbrush/spraycan or water droplet to add an effect
Free choice	Use a cloning tool to duplicate a part of the image
Posterise the image to four levels	Use a number of distorting filters
Choose an embossing filter with different levels of embossing in different parts	Free choice
Use a mask to colour an area in a solid colour	Fill a part of the image with a pattern of your own
Perform a gradient blend	Alter the brightness and contracts of the image
Free choice	Adjust the levels of R, G and B for the image

Figure 16.2 Task cards

Paper sizes are all based on the aspect ratio of the square root of 2, or approximately 1 : 1.41 with the base A0 size of paper defined as having an area of 1 m². Rounded to the nearest millimetre, A0 paper size is 841 mm by 1189 mm. Use this fact to calculate the size of an A1 sheet and an A4 sheet from Figure 16.3.

9780170411813

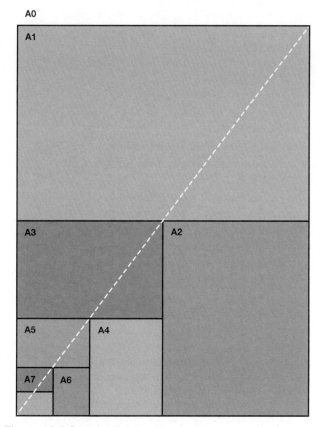

A0

A1

A3

A2

A5

A4

A7

A6

Figure 16.3 Standardised paper sizes

1 Use the Internet to acquire a copyright-free image or even better, photograph one yourself. It is important that the photo is at sufficient resolution to allow for enlargement.
2 Enlarge your image to A1 size using Photoshop. Use a smaller screen-size percentage to view the whole image on your monitor.

3 Lucky-dip from the eight tasks to perform on the image. Your teacher will either show you how to perform each task or ask you to use the Internet to discover how to achieve it. Practise first!

Designing

1 Divide your single image in the pattern of eight equal-sized A4 pages and save each section with image names containing the letters 'A', 'B', 'C', 'D', 'E', 'F', 'G', 'H' and 'I'. Make sure each of these is sized to A4.
2 Maintain the *aspect ratio* of each in relation to the paper you will print on and its orientation. Consider the size of each image – make sure it is set to an A4 sheet of paper. It may be necessary to trim the final printout before assembling your mural.

Implementing

1 Perform the assigned lucky-dip tasks on separate images. Keep track of the order.
2 Add text as labels to describe the effects you used on each section.
3 Print your pages in colour. Assemble them loosely on the floor to create your A1 sized mural.

Evaluating

1 Examine your results and suggest improvements.
2 When you are satisfied with your mural, laminate each one, if possible. Join the images using heavy tape on the reverse. Hang a plastic sheet in front if you are unable to laminate.
3 Fix your mural to the wall with a copy of the original. The murals become an art exhibition for the class to evaluate. The class evaluates each mural using the template in Table 16.1.

Table 16.1

Mural name	Design skills /5	Technical skills /5	Total /10

1 What did you learn by completing this project?

_____

_____

_____

_____

_____

2 Identify additional features you could include.

_____

_____

_____

_____

_____

17 PROJECT: COMPARING WEBSITE BUILDERS

THE TASK

Your task is to compare an online 'drag and drop' website builder with a dedicated website design authoring tool by creating a portfolio to display your digital technology work, using the same content for each tool.

Website builders allow the design of websites without manual coding. In *Digital Technologies 9 & 10*, you will learn to code a website manually using HTML, CSS and JavaScript coding.

You will compare online builders that use predefined templates to an application where you create your own design.

Shutterstock.com/Mmaxer

Web tools come in three 'flavours'

Basic: Websites providing predefined features and templates (such as Wix, Squarespace or Weebly).
Intermediate: Design-based tools (such as Adobe Muse CC).
Advanced: Hand-coded sites using CSS and JavaScript (e.g. Dreamweaver, along with its responsive inclusion Bootstrap).

To code or not to code?

It is helpful to design a website before attempting to manually code using CSS, HTML and JavaScript.

Using a web-design tool rather than a web-coding tool for your first web design project will help you later on in Years 9 and 10 to master the Australian Curriculum outcome, 'Design the user experience of a digital system

by evaluating alternative designs against criteria including functionality, accessibility, usability, and aesthetics' (ACTDIP039). AC

Digital Technologies 9 & 10 features a web design coding project if you want to tackle HTML, CSS and JavaScript immediately. Grok Learning, Code academy and W3Schools tutorials are recommended. Weblinks provided at the *Digital Technologies 7 & 8* website.

Weblink

INFOBIT: FIXED DESIGN

For many years, following the launch of HTML in 1991, websites used fixed layouts. Web designers often used tables to lay out their text and graphics.

When small-screen devices arrived, websites looked terrible when squeezed into different proportions and web designers needed three versions of their sites: one for desktop, tablet and phone.

Adaptive design
Adaptive design meant web designers could more easily create three different versions of their websites, and browsers would display the correct version.

Responsive design
Responsive web design tools now use coding to control the design and content for scaling to different screen sizes. Designers need to create only one layout.

Defining

You need to select two web builders for this project.
* Select a free web-builder tool with built-in templates. (Suggestions are either Weebly, Wix or Squarespace.)
* Select a drag and drop web tool where you create your own design, such as Adobe Muse CC.

Consider the following questions and prompts:
* Who is your audience?
* Conduct research into designs on the web.
* Identify the features you like of the examples you've found during your research.
* What media types will you include (text, audio, images, animation, video)?
* What method will you use to indicate links (underlined text, roll-over features [image swell or highlighting, audio feedback])?

9780170411813

Designing

Create or acquire assets for your website. Remember that images must be either jpeg, gif or png (see Table 2.9 in Chapter 2). Plan a storyboard representing the site map of the website, showing all pages and navigation between them. Label the pages with descriptions of the content that will appear on each.

Figure 17.1 shows an example to give you ideas. Follow these steps:

- Choose to sketch a site map on paper or use a mind mapping tool, such as MindNode or FreeMind. Paper sketches can offer more creative freedom!
- Decide the main (first level) pages.
- Decide the second level pages (avoid creating third levels here).
- Sketch links.
- Select a template to use from those provided for free online.
- Sketch your own design.
- Select a colour palette.

Web builder with built-in design templates

For the predefined web-builder tool, select one of their templates.

Sketch the layout of the supplied template you have chosen, showing all links between pages. Use your website design to guide you in adding text, images and links to the built-in template you have chosen.

Drag and drop web builder tool using your own design

We recommend Adobe Muse as a suitable tool here.

Visit the Adobe Muse website and select the Learning link where you will find excellent Beginner video guides and online tutorials. Complete the beginner tutorials before commencing your own site in the following section.

Implementing

1 Create a folder for your website.
2 Inside this folder, place all the digital assets required for this project in a second folder called 'Images'.
3 Build your website using a web builder with the predefined template.
4 Build your website again using the drag and drop web builder and your own design.
5 Which approach did you prefer?

_____

_____

_____

_____

Evaluating

1 Check the appearances of the two websites on a smartphone, tablet, laptop and desktop.
2 Make changes based on suggestions by class members.
3 Rate each web builder against features listed in Table 17.1 on the next page and calculate a score for each.
4 Which of the two approaches would you choose next time you had to design a personal portfolio? Why?

_____

_____

_____

_____

_____

_____

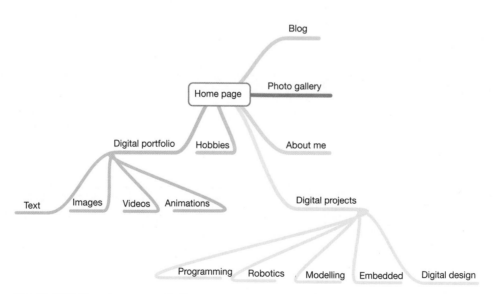

Figure 17.1 Planning your website

Table 17.1

| Feature | Max score | Comparing two web builders | |
		Predefined template web builder	Drag and drop web builder
Ease of use	5		
Design	5		
User experience	5		
Responsive design? (Automatically adjusts web pages to device screen size)	3		
E-commerce	2		
Blogging	2		
Customisable using HTML/CSS	2		
Free to use	2		
Free domain name	2		
Level of support	2		
Final result	5		
Additional features	5		
Final score	**40**		

5 What did you learn by completing this project?

_____

_____

_____

_____

_____

_____

_____

_____

6 Identify additional features you could include.

_____

_____

_____

_____

_____

_____

_____

_____

7 What changes would you make to your design?

_____

_____

_____

_____

_____

_____

_____

_____

_____

_____

_____

_____

_____

9780170411813

PROJECT: CHOOSE-YOUR-OWN-ADVENTURE WEBSITE

18

THE TASK

Your task is to create an adventure where readers choose their own path. Your interactive storybook will be in the form of a website.

This project presumes you have previously completed a website project and are familiar with the technical and design skills required. The previous chapter introduces these skills: Comparing website builders.

You may choose to add animations and interactive game elements if you want.

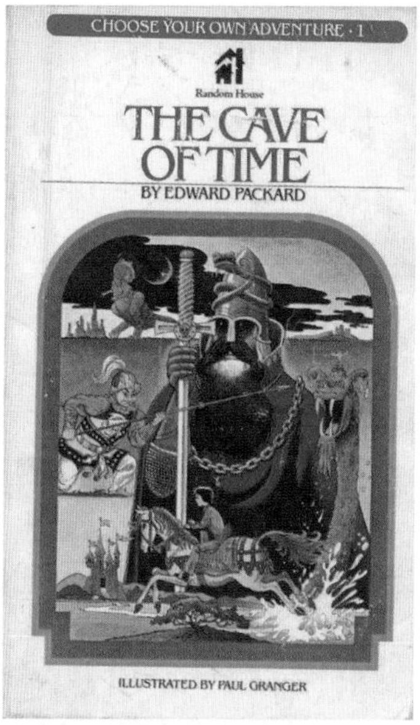

Figure 18.1 The first choose-your-own-adventure book, published in 1979

Edward Packard told his daughters made-up bedtime stories every night. He said that one night he ran out of ideas so he just asked his daughter what the character would do. His two daughters came up with different ideas and so he thought of an ending for each. After being rejected by many publishers, his books ended up selling 250 million copies!

> **INFOBIT**
>
> Before interactive digital entertainment, choose-your-own-adventure books were an early popular interactive entertainment.

Threaded choose-your-own-adventure stories can be exciting. The author puts the reader 'in control' of the plot. One challenge, however, is that every time a choice is added, the author has to write more!

Choose-your-own-adventure books have pages that look like Figure 18.2.

> 4 ***The old man***
>
> You had seen the old man every day on the way to school. He sat on his front verandah, holding his newspaper, mostly ignoring you but sometimes giving you slightest nod ... so slight that you had to guess if you had seen his head move at all.
>
> You know this house well as it is right beside the community hall and you wonder how it could have been allowed to be run down so seriously. It needs a paint job – or just demolition.
> Then one day the old man isn't on his verandah any more.
> Or the following day.
>
> Or the next.
>
> You see into a room through the front window from the street. You notice a pile of newspapers that seemed to stretch halfway up the wall, and you can see piles of what seem like dirty plates piled unsteadily on a table.
>
> For two weeks you walk past the house and the empty verandah. Nothing changes. From the back of the hall you see the rear door is open. You realise you can climb the fence easily and just walk in.
>
> *If you decide to climb the fence and enter the house go to page 10*
>
> *If you decide to knock on the front door go to page 15*

Figure 18.2 A typical page from a choose your own adventure book. You decide which adventure you want!

A website is a perfect digital tool to create an online version of the printed books as the user has to click a choice and cannot cheat before choosing their response!

Defining

Find some examples online of choose-your-own-adventure stories and gather some ideas before commencing this project. Some website versions allow users to invent their own branches to extend the adventures.

An important thing to notice is that these stories are written in the second-person narrative ('you'), as in the story in Figure 18.2.

Designing

1 Create a storyboard that will become a navigational diagram for your website. For this type of project, it will be similar to the one shown in Figure 18.3, which has a *hierarchical* structure. Sketch out a rough version of your adventure story using bullet points and arrange the story, perhaps using a table where the columns double each row. Your story plan should look similar to the structure shown in Table 18.1 and Figure 18.3.
2 Invent at least two branching decisions where users can choose what direction they will take in the story by clicking hyperlinks. This would create four different adventures. Have the teacher approve your storyboard.
3 Choose the web design tool you will use.
4 Acquire or create any text, graphics, videos or background designs.
    If you have created a story using still images, consider adding animations.

Producing

1 Create all the pages of your website, including all text, images, animations and videos.
2 Create interactivity by adding hyperlinks and anchors.

3 Create decision points where readers will choose between destinations. Each of these will take the story in a different direction.

Evaluating

1 Perform repeated testing with users and improve your story, repeating the design sequence.
2 What did you learn by completing this project?

_____

_____

_____

_____

_____

_____

3 Identify additional features you could include.

_____

_____

_____

_____

_____

_____

_____

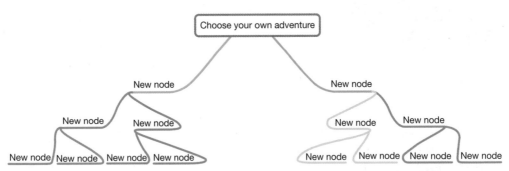

Figure 18.3 The hierarchical structure for a choose-your-own-adventure book, shown as a diagram

Table 18.1 The hierarchical structure for a choose-your-own-adventure book, shown as a table

Old man disappears from old house							
Choose: climb fence and enter open door				*Choose: knock on front door*			
Hear strange noise from lounge room				No answer but door seems slightly open			
Choose: move towards lounge room		*Choose: scared so leave and invite a friend*		*Choose: open door and enter*		*Choose: scared so leave and invite a friend*	
Next part of story		Next part of story		Next part of story		Next part of story	
Choice 1	*Choice 2*	*Choice 1*	*Choice 2*	*Choice 1*	*Choice 2*	*Choice 1*	*Choice 2*
Next part of story	Next part of story	Next part of story	Next part of story	Next part of story	Next part of story	Next part of story	Next part of story

19

THE TASK

Your task is to design and print your own 3D object.

Using high-end three-dimensional design software can be a steep learning curve. The idea of this task is for you to dip your toes into 3D design by using the free application SketchUp Make to create a house. Then, if you have access to a 3D printer, to print it.

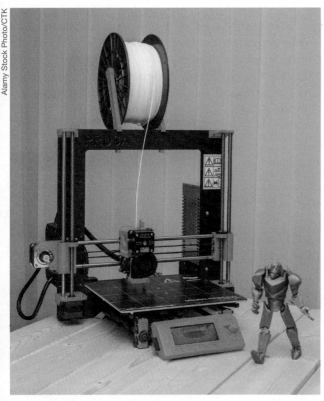

Figure 19.1 The Prusa i3 3D printer

Of course, you can always just download a 3D file from a website, such as Thingiverse, but that means you do not learn how to create anything yourself. If you like what you see, there's an even bigger world to explore. Some possibilities are suggested at the end of this chapter.

Guided project: Build a house

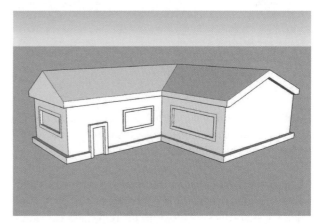

Figure 19.2a Final 3D model of a house using SketchUp Make

SketchUp Make is used to illustrate the steps briefly below, but you may need to ask your teacher to demonstrate these in greater detail or use an online tutorial. If you need more help, a similar activity is outlined in Part 2 of the 'Getting started with SketchUp' tutorial series found on the SketchUp website.

1   Create two adjacent rectangles and erase the joining line (see Figure 19.2b).

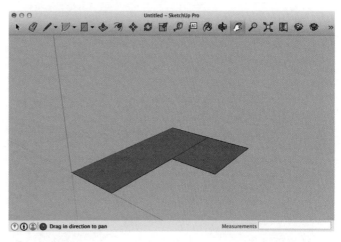

Figure 19.2b

2 Lift this base using the Push/Pull tool (see Figure 19.2c).

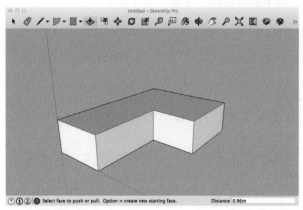

Figure 19.2c

3 Find the centre of the top front edge (a blue dot), click once and let go, then hover over the centre of the right back edge (until a blue dot appears) but do not click. Hover the mouse pointer near the centre of the ridge and click when SketchUp identifies this central position. Then click the centre of the right edge to complete the ridge. Use the Line tool to draw the remaining two short diagonal ridge lines (see Figure 19.2d).

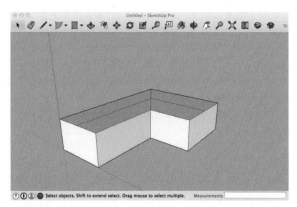

Figure 19.2d

4 Shift-select this new centre ridge and lift using the Move tool (see Figure 19.2e).

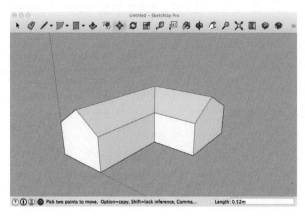

Figure 19.2e

5 Use the Orbit tool to look underneath your house and use the Offset tool to create an inset (see Figure 19.2f).

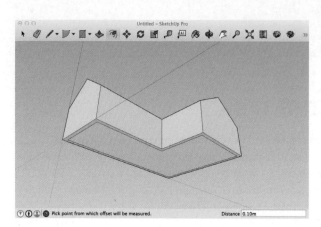

Figure 19.2f

6 Use the Push/Pull tool to lift this border to form the overhang of the roof. Use the Follow Me tool to create a ridge around the base of your house (ask your teacher for help if required here). Add doors and windows (using one or two insets). Finally, add materials as required (see Figure 19.2g).

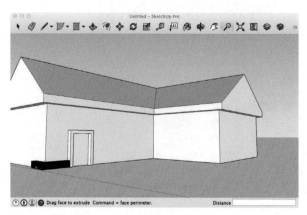

Figure 19.2g

7 Complete your software 3D house model by using SketchUp Make to add materials to its surfaces (see Figure 19.2h).

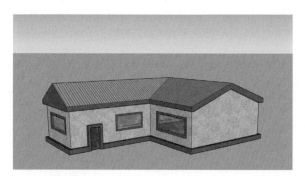

Figure 19.2h

8   Optional: If you are printing a 3D-printed version, you need to install the free .stl SketchUp export plug-in (easily located on the web).
9   Export (under File) your file in 3D .obj or .stl format and then import it to your printer's software. (This is shown placed on the build platform of MakerBot 3D printer's application.) Then 3D-print your house (see Figure 19.2i).

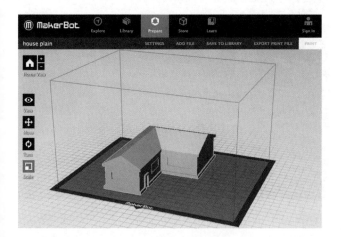

Figure 19.2i Top: House on printer software's virtual build platform. Bottom: Final 3D printed house.

PROJECT IDEAS: CREATE YOUR OWN PUZZLE

Try to create one of the following 3D puzzles. Use any suitable 3D design tool. 3D design software suggestions:
- 3D Tin
- 123D Design
- TinkerCAD
- SketchUp.

Classic tangram

1   Search the web to find the exact dimensions of the seven pieces for the classic tangram puzzle (Figure 19.3).
2   Create them and print a set.

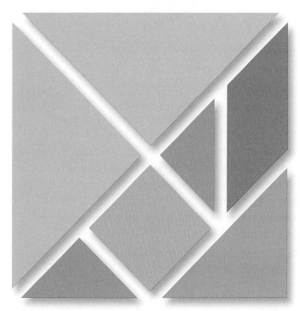

Figure 19.3 The classic tangram puzzle

Web probe: Applications of 3D printing

1   Search online for 'En-able' and summarise how 3D printers are used to produce the parts for artificial limbs.

_____

_____

_____

2   Discover three other uses of 3D printing that significantly benefit society.

_____

_____

_____

Secret marble maze

1 Design and print a maze (Figure 19.4) with an escape hole for a small marble.
2 Add a lid to hide the secret.

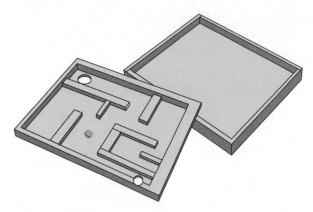

Figure 19.4 Marble maze

Soma cube

Figure 19.6 A final 3D printed version of the soma cube.

The pieces of the soma cube consist of all possible combinations of three or four unit cubes, joined at their faces with at least one inside corner. These seven puzzle pieces fit together to form a cube. Their shapes can be identified by letters whose shapes they resemble, and are shown in Figure 19.5.

1 Create and print these cubes along with a box (and lid) they fit in.

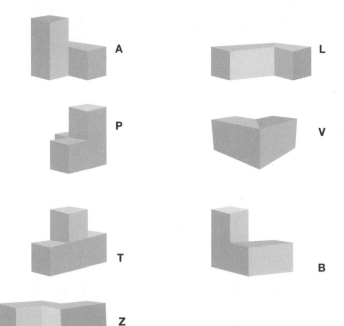

Figure 19.5 The soma cube puzzle

9780170411813

GUIDED PROJECT: INFORMATION SYSTEMS AND DATABASES

database An organised collection of data comprising files, records and fields. Database structures allow ease of access, management and searching of data

field Discrete piece of stored data (for example, song title, song artist or bank account number)

primary key A primary key is a field in a table that is unique. It can be used to uniquely identify every record and is often a serial number

record Values in collection of fields associated with an entity (for example, a song, a bank transaction)

validation Checks for the correctness and meaningfulness of data input to the system

Of all the types of software that influence our daily life, databases have the most impact. Even Google is an example of a (very big!) **database**. Yet most people know little about them. For you, this is about to change!

Understanding data has become more important than ever in society. Knowing about information systems and databases is important for managing your own data and understanding how to protect your privacy.

Following are some typical examples of information systems using databases.

Biometric security devices use biological characteristics to identify people. How does the computer know which person the data belongs to?

Computers use specialised input devices to read information stored as optical marks, barcodes and special characters. Where would you see examples of this type of data?

Data collected in the workshop is transferred to the main database that keeps track of parts used.

Specialised terminals like this one make it easy to log restaurant orders. How has the nature of this person's work changed as a result of technology?

Couriers use pen-based computers to log deliveries and record signatures.

Figure 20.1 Data is collected from a wide variety of sources for storage in databases.

Information systems and databases

An information system is a combination of hardware and software components, data, processes and people that interact to create, control and communicate information.

A database is an example of the software part of an information system.

WHAT IS A DATABASE?

A database is an organised collection of related data.

A simple database consists of files, made up of **records**, which are made up of **fields**.

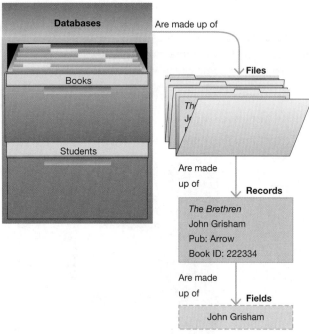

Figure 20.2 A database is like an electronic filing cabinet.

For example, in a library, all books have an author, a title, a publisher and an ISBN (international standard book number). These items are fields and together they form a record for a single book.

Lots of these records form the catalogue file for the library.

To start building a database, you might think of collecting several items of data about one particular idea or project or topic (fields), and organising them into a table.

It is important that you include a field in each table or file to hold a unique code for each record. This field is called a **primary key**. A library may have several copies of the same title, or two books may have similar names. If each physical book has a unique number code or ID, it cannot be confused with any other.

Types of databases

Flat file databases use a single table of data. Relational databases connect more than one table together.

By organising data in separate tables, you can more easily manage it. Think about the school library. You could create a table of data about the books, plus a table of data about the borrowers. A third table could record loans by students. These obviously have different types of data, so you can build separate tables. You then link tables so that you can display details about book each student has on loan.

Here we focus on flat file databases. In *Digital Technologies 9 & 10*, we focus on relational databases and searching using a language called SQL.

Google search is really a huge database. It uses its own unique database structure.

Database design

Your task

Two common applications used for building databases are Microsoft Access and FileMaker Pro.

To better understand databases, this guided task will help you build a simple flat-file database.

In the next project in Chapter 21 you will create a more complex flat-file database, and in *Digital Technologies 9 & 10* you will create a relational database.

The following are some fields you might need:
- project title
- project code (a unique primary key)
- topic
- type of project: group, individual, either
- date commenced
- date completed
- result
- comments.

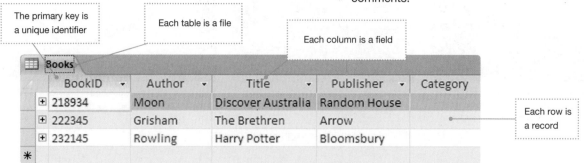

Figure 20.3 A simple database is a collection of data organised by defining records and fields.

9780170411813

Most of these are in the form of text or numbers.

A database needs to be able to arrange or sort data and so you need to tell the database what type of data each field is. This is because numbers, text and dates, for example, are sorted differently.

A common mistake is to define fields containing phone numbers as number fields. What field type do you think phone numbers should be? Why?

1 Open your database software and create a new file. Save it using the name 'Projects'.
2 Often a field will only have an entry from a restricted set of values, such as the states of Australia. You can create a graphical control called a *dropdown list* (See Figures 20.4 and 20.5). This eliminates typos. Other common graphical controls are *radio buttons* and *check boxes*.

Although you originally defined 'type of project' as a text field, you will only ever use a fixed list of three terms to describe the type of project: group, individual or either. This means the most suitable input control for the 'type of project' field will be a dropdown menu.

Create the fields shown in Table 20.1.

Table 20.1 Defining the fields. Note: the project code field is omitted in the following figures.

Field name	Field type	Graphical control element
Project title	Text	Standard textbox
Project code	Number (unique)	Automatically generated
Topic	Text	Standard textbox
Type of project: group, individual, either	Text	Dropdown list
Completed	Boolean	Radio button
Date commenced	Date	Standard textbox (date)
Date completed	Date	Standard textbox (date)
Result	Number	Standard textbox
Comments	Text	Standard textbox

3 Create a dropdown list for 'type of project' and assign it to that field (Figure 20.4).

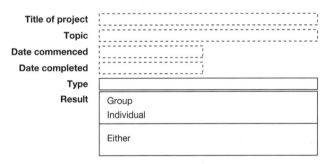

Figure 20.4 Defining a dropdown list

Now when users try to enter data, only three choices appear in the dropdown (Figure 20.5).

Figure 20.5 Data entry using dropdown menu

Populating a database

1 Entering data in a database is described as *populating* it. Populate your new database with the following records. When you have finished entering these, your database table will appear as shown in Table 20.2.

Table 20.2

Project database					
Title of project	**Topic**	**Date commenced**	**Date completed**	**Type of project**	**Result**
Robo Olympics	Robotics	15/6/2018	12/7/2018	Group	78
Text-based adventure	Programming	2/4/2018	6/5/2018	Individual	67
Who wants to be a millionaire?	Modelling, simulation	2/8/2018	30/8/2018	Individual	91
Human rights	Multimedia	2/10/2018	4/11/2018	Group	82
Convict database	Databases	1/5/2018	15/5/2018	Either	82

2 Sort the records in descending order of marks (see under 'result' in Table 20.3).

Table 20.3

Project database					
Title of project	**Topic**	**Date commenced**	**Date completed**	**Type of project**	**Result**
Who wants to be a millionaire?	Modelling, simulation	2/8/2018	30/8/2018	Individual	91
Convict database	Databases	1/5/2018	15/5/2018	Either	82
Human rights	Multimedia	2/10/2018	4/11/2018	Group	82
Robo Olympics	Robotics	15/6/2018	12/7/2018	Group	78
Text-based adventure	Programming	2/4/2018	6/5/2018	Individual	67

The highest result mark will appear first: 91, for 'Who wants to be a millionaire?'.

3 Sort the records by the date commenced order by clicking the heading for that column. The first record should be 2/4/2018, called 'Text-based adventure'. This will only be sorted correctly if the Date commenced field is defined properly as the date data type. See Table 20.4.

Table 20.4

Project database					
Title of project	**Topic**	**Date commenced**	**Date completed**	**Type of project**	**Result**
Text-based adventure	Programming	2/4/2018	6/5/2018	Individual	67
Convict database	Databases	1/5/2018	15/5/2018	Either	82
Robo Olympics	Robotics	15/6/2018	12/7/2018	Group	78
Who wants to be a millionaire?	Modelling, simulation	2/8/2018	30/8/2018	Individual	91
Human rights	Multimedia	2/10/2018	4/11/2018	Group	82

Searching a database

The secret search power of a database can now be revealed. Real databases can have many millions of entries.
Imagine you want to find all the projects for which you were awarded more than 80 marks.

1 Enter Find mode for your database and enter a search for the Result field as '>80'.
This will return three records, all of which have been awarded a mark greater than 80. See Table 20.5.

Table 20.5 Search results for 'Result > 80'

5/11/2018	Project database				
Title of project	**Topic**	**Date commenced**	**Date completed**	**Type of project**	**Result**
Convict database	Databases	1/5/2018	15/5/2018	Either	82
Who wants to be a millionaire?	Modelling, simulation	2/8/2018	30/8/2018	Individual	91
Human rights	Multimedia	2/10/2018	4/11/2018	Group	82

Databases also offer more complex searches.
After searching any database it is always important to show all records again before continuing.

2 Search for projects that received a mark greater than 80 and were 'Database projects'. What is your result?

9780170411813

Database reports

Table 20.6 A database report

5/11/2018	Project database				
Title of project	**Topic**	**Date commenced**	**Date completed**	**Type of project**	**Result**
Text-based adventure	Programming	2/4/2018	6/5/2018	Individual	67
Convict database	Databases	1/5/2018	15/5/2018	Either	82
Robo Olympics	Robotics	15/6/2018	12/7/2018	Group	78
Who wants to be a millionaire?	Modelling, simulation	2/8/2018	30/8/2018	Individual	91
Human rights	Multimedia	2/10/2018	4/11/2018	Group	82
				Overall average	80

When you need to present data, a report allows you to select the data to display.

Both Microsoft Access and FileMaker Pro include report-maker tools.

Reports allow you to add titles, dates and even calculations and summaries of parts of your data.

1. In Microsoft Access, use the tab Create > Report. Then use the Format tab and the Design tab to make adjustments to your report's appearance.
   In FileMaker Pro, choose Layouts > New layout and select the Columnar list/report style. Respond to the dialogue boxes, the last of which asks you to select one of a number of templates for your report.
2. Notice the 'overall average' mark of 80 displayed at the base of this report in Table 20.6? Create this, place it and add a summary part to the end of your report layout.

Evaluation

1. What did you learn by completing this project?

_____

_____

_____

_____

_____

2. Identify additional features you could include in your database.

_____

_____

_____

_____

Advanced: Validation and calculation data

Database applications allow designers to set up **validation** checks on data to check if it is reasonable. For example, if you tried to enter a date completed that was earlier than the date commenced, a validation rule could reject it.

1. Set up a validation rule for your database. You will write a rule such as Date completed occurs after Date commenced.
   In Microsoft Access, On the Fields tab, in the Field Validation group, click Validation and set up your rule.
   In FileMaker Pro, in File> Define > Database click Fields tab. Click Options. Click Validation and set up your rule.
2. It is also easy to define calculation fields. To try this out, create a calculation field to turn the marks out of 100 listed here to integer marks out of 20, rounded to nearest integer.

Figure 20.6 Data warehouses are servers that store large volumes of data not needed immediately, or data they are sharing with other organisations.

21 PROJECT: CLASS DATABASE

THE TASK

Your task is to design your own class database. Class members move from computer to computer and enter data. You then analyse data to interpret class data and produce a report on your discoveries.

Before you start this task you will explore existing, free online tools for data collection and analysis.

ConCensus (ABC Splash)

This website allows you to explore Australian Bureau of Statistics (ABS) data, then design and generate your own MyCensus (with a shareable URL) by selecting questions from the following categories: personal and family details, language and culture, recreation and entertainment, eating and sleeping, getting to school, technology, friends, travel and interests, society and the environment, and the future – personal, technological.

A link to the ConCensus website has been provided at the *Digital Technologies 7 & 8* website.

Weblink

1   Visit the ConCensus website and create a MyCensus for your class, using a limit of five questions.
2   The class will need to set up a collaborative website to post MyCensus URLs.
3   Class members fill in each person's survey.
4   Analyse your MyCensus results using the built-in tools.
5   Record one thing you discovered about your class from your MyCensus.

_____

_____

_____

_____

_____

_____

_____

_____

_____

Activity: SurveyMonkey

SurveyMonkey is a well-known website for creating online surveys. Visit SurveyMonkey and summarise differences between the free version and the paid version. Does the free version of SurveyMonkey allow data to be downloaded to a database?

Skill builder

_____

_____

_____

_____

_____

_____

_____

_____

Defining

Your task is to design your own database that class members will populate with their data. Start with a class discussion on the following issues:

* What questions do you want a class database to answer?
* What is one positive purpose of your database, apart from students learning to use databases?
* Could your database be misused:
    - by a student?
    - by a teacher?
    - by an adult visiting the computer room after class?
    - online by an unauthorised person?
* Could the database be protected from unauthorised use? How?
* What are other ideas for suitable fields?
* Are any suggested fields inappropriate? Why?
* Should some fields be optional? Which ones?
* Should some fields be compulsory? Which ones?
* Discuss database user terms such as functionality, accessibility and aesthetics.
* What criteria make a database technically excellent?
* What criteria make a database excellent in design and user-friendliness?

Your database could include basic fields, such as:

- gender
- year of enrolment at present school
- country of birth
- languages spoken
- life milestones
- favourite subject
- music
- hobby
- sporting interests
- life goal
- greatest strength
- primary key: serial number unique to each entry (the student ID number).

Designing

Consider the following:

1 Decide which fields you will use.
2 Consider possible design and layout approaches. Sketch a layout for the records. Consider carefully the positioning of fields on the screen for data entry.
3 What are the appropriate data types of each field?
   - Determine pre-defined dropdown lists.
   - Consider use of radio buttons and check boxes.
   - Require that some fields need to have unique entries.
   - Require that some fields can never be left empty.
   - Require that one field will give the student ID as a serial number with an increment of 1. Suggestion is to start at 'YYYYXXXX', where YYYY indicates the current year and XXXX is a serial number.
4 What is the tab order of fields (look this up if you need to)?
5 What type of reports are likely to be required? What fields require sorts performed on them?
6 Prepare an evaluation sheet as per the example shown in Table 21.1 and add enough rows for the number of students in your class.
   Your database will be peer evaluated based on two skills: technical and design.

Table 21.1 Database evaluation sheet 1 = low, 5 = high

Technical 1–5	Design 1–5	List one strength	Suggest one improvement

Implementing

1 Build your database.
2 After all the class designs have been completed, print the evaluation sheet and place in front of the monitor of your computer.
3 Move from computer to computer, entering your own details into each student database around the classroom. Record a score between 1 to 5 for **technical** and 1 to 5 for **design** on each evaluation sheet.

Evaluating

1 After all students have entered their details and recorded their marks for all databases, return to your database and total your score. Circle suggested improvements on your evaluation sheet.
2 Have a class discussion to determine which features made some databases easier to use or more enjoyable.
3 Improve your database in response to the suggestions from peer feedback.
4 Produce a report for your teacher, using your database to uncover interesting discoveries about your classmates.
5 Following are some ideas for interesting discoveries, but you can make up your own.
   - Most popular school subject.
   - Favourite subjects with the total number of students that chose each.
   - Most popular female hobby versus most popular male hobby.
   - Most common country of birth.
   - Proportion of students who speak more than one language.
6 What did you learn from this project?

_____

_____

_____

_____

7 Identify additional features you could include in your database.

_____

_____

_____

_____

_____

22

PROJECT: ADVENTURES IN DATA DIVING

Around the room are five data-based activities. Your task is to complete any four in any order, in a group or individually, then to prepare a presentation on what you have learnt about data analysis.

- Task A   Word and data clouds
- Task B   Infographics
- Task C   Run that town
- Task D   Data and artificial intelligence
- Task E   Data and pattern recognition

Weblink

TASK A: WORD AND DATA CLOUDS

In this task you will use cloud generators as an information system for data analysis.

A word cloud (or tag cloud) is a visual display of the most common words in a collection of text. The words that occur most often are written using a larger font.

Below are two word clouds, generated from text in the class database project.

Word clouds have been used by historians to compare speeches, such as the important State of the Union speeches given by Presidents of the United States.

1   Form groups of four people. Each person investigates one of the following tools and completes Table 22.1:

- Wordle
- WordItOut
- TagCrowd
- Tagzedo
- Word Cloud Generator (an add-on in Google docs).

Figure 22.1 Two word clouds, generated by Wordle, using identical data, based on the text in the class database chapter (Chapter 21). Which five words are used the most often? It is not surprising that the most common word is 'databases'!

Table 22.1

Tool used:

Issue	My evaluation
Interface	
Usability	
Speed	
Accuracy (use test case text)	
Output presentation	
Is it customisable?	
Does it cost? Is it ad-free?	
Additional features	
Desired missing features	

2   Use your word cloud tool to compare one of the following:
   - State of the Union speeches by former American President Barack Obama and by current President Donald Trump.
   - Speeches by two different Australian politicians.
   - Reports by different newspapers of the same event.

3   Discuss with another class member what programming and interface issues the designer of a word cloud generator would need to consider. Consider words like 'the' and 'a' and the same word with different endings such as 'promise' and 'promised'. Add issues in dot points to Table 22.2.

Table 22.2

Programming issues	Interface issues

A data cloud uses font sizes and colours to represent numbers. It is similar to a word cloud, but instead of using word counts it displays data such as population or stock market prices.

4   Figure 22.2 is a word cloud of countries according to population. What information does this image reveal?

_____

_____

_____

_____

_____

Figure 22.2

5   Discuss your data analysis as a group.
6   What are the strengths and weaknesses of cloud generators for data analysis?

_____

_____

_____

_____

_____

_____

_____

TASK B: INFOGRAPHICS

In this task you will design an infographic. An infographic is a visual representation of data. Animated infographics are used widely in TV presentations.

1   Search the web for examples of infographics and identify styles you like. Think about what it is that you like about them. Select a topic from the list below:
    • the anatomy of a hamburger
    • a breakdown of parts for a smartphone
    • laptop ownership among students
    • why you should visit (country)
    • choose your own.

2   Try out each of the following free online tools for creating infographics:
    • Easel.ly
    • Infogr.am
    • Piktochart.

3   Choose a built-in template.
4   Replace images and graphs as required. Double-click on graph placeholders to edit data.
5   Optional: print your chart in colour.

TASK C: RUN THAT TOWN

Your task is to play the free Australian Bureau of Statistics (ABS) game 'Run that Town' (iOS only) and evaluate how successful the ABS was in achieving the goal outlined below.

The Australian Bureau of Statistics was looking for ways to get people more engaged with Census data, to help them understand why data matters and how it can help guide planning and policy decisions. The goal was to create an engaging way people could use the data for themselves, so they created a mobile game that lets people take charge of their actual suburb – using real census data from their town.

Figure 22.3

1 Play the game for at least 30 minutes. How successful do you think the ABS were? What are the strengths and weaknesses of the game?

_____

_____

_____

_____

_____

_____

TASK D: DATA AND ARTIFICIAL INTELLIGENCE

20Q.net.Inc

Figure 22.4

20Q is a toy that can be physically handheld, or played as an online toy. Visit the 20Q website and use the 'classic' setting to play the game five times. The online version of 20Q guesses correctly about 80 per cent of the time, and if you allow it 25 questions, it claims a 98 per cent success rate.

Start with the object 'candle'. Once 20Q has guessed this object, think of your own.

1 How do you think the software recognises the objects you are thinking of? Read the information on the FAQ link and describe below how the game works.

_____

_____

_____

_____

_____

_____

2 It has been said 'Big Data + Artificial Intelligence = Boom!'. Explain below what this might mean.

_____

_____

_____

_____

_____

_____

_____

TASK E: PATTERN RECOGNITION

Quick, Draw!

Quick, Draw! is an online Google artificial intelligence (AI) experiment where you are given an object to draw and the software then tries to guess your drawing. The more you play, the more it learns. Search for it online. Attempts are made to match your drawing to patterns from previous ones. Quick, Draw! not only looks at your drawing's shape, but also at which strokes you make first and the direction you make them.

Google and the Google logo are registered trademarks of Google Inc., used with permission.

Can a neural network learn to recognize doodles?

Help teach it by adding your drawings to the world's largest doodle data set, which could be shared publicly to help with machine learning research in the future.

Figure 22.5

1   Find a partner and play the game five times each. Which of you had the higher success rate? This Google AI experiment works using a neural network. Find out what this is and describe it below.

_____

_____

_____

_____

_____

2   Imagine five ways in which this technology could be used effectively.

Table 22.3

1	
2	
3	
4	
5	

Image recognition

1   Download two different free image recognition apps for your mobile device. (*TapTapSee* and *CamFind* are two suggestions.)
2   Compare the apps by performing a test using 10 different images and complete the table.

Table 22.4

Item	App 1	App 2

Item	App 1	App 2

3 Compare the accuracy, functionality and interfaces of the two apps. Which do you prefer and why?

_____

_____

4 Most mobile device personal photo libraries are searchable using image recognition by typing a search word, such as 'tree' (e.g. Apple iOS Photos). Try searching for photos of food in an image library on your mobile device or a computer. Complete Table 22.5, testing four other categories.

Table 22.5

Test object	Total responses	Number falsely identified	Percentage correct

App tested: _____

TASK F: PRESENTATION

Prepare a presentation to the class summarising what you have learnt about the strengths and weaknesses of data analysis from completing the previous activities. Consider issues of privacy and data security.

GLOSSARY

actuator Output devices, such as motors that convert signals into movement

robot Machine able to perform tasks automatically

robotics The science of the use and study of robots

sensor Input device that accepts data from the environment

In this guided project you will be introduced to two types of programmable robots, which you will learn to control using simple code. In the following chapters you will extend these skills using more advanced activities.

Note: it will be helpful to complete Chapter 3 before commencing this unit.

Robotics is the science of the use and study of **robots**. The term 'robot' is usually applied to a machine able to perform tasks automatically. These tasks can range from making cars to defusing bombs.

A robot can perform tasks that are repetitive, tedious, dangerous, very precise or even impossible for people to undertake. Robots have the advantage of never getting tired, being able to work with much higher accuracy than humans and even being able to do things that humans cannot do, such as working in extreme temperatures.

A BRIEF HISTORY

In the 15th century, Leonardo da Vinci, a famous Italian mathematician, artist and designer, drew plans for robots, although he did not use this word. He designed a mediaeval knight and a drumming robot designed to keep a perfect beat once its handle had been wound.

During the 1920s, a playwright named Karel Capek wrote about a factory that produced mechanical devices called 'robota', the Czech word for work, which gave us the word robot. In his play, the robots eventually take over the world.

The earliest robots were built specifically to perform simple tasks on an assembly line and are still widely used in manufacturing.

Modern robots usually have **sensors** to accept data from the environment. Their inputs may include senses of vision, touch, hearing and smell.

Newspix/Charles Brewer

Figure 23.1 Leonardo da Vinci's drumming robot, created by engineer Gabriele Niccolai from da Vinci's sketches

Humans continue to be fascinated by robots. Over the years, robots have featured in many TV series and movies, including *2001: A Space Odyssey*, *Star Wars*, *iRobot* and *Transformers*.

PROGRAMMABLE ROBOTS

The Ozobot

The Ozobot robot is an afforable, powerful programmable robot but you won't need one to complete this activity.

This robot is about the size of a golf ball and has impressive features: it can be charged by USB and programs are loaded by holding the robot up to a flashing coloured spot on the screen of a computer (or tablet)!

Figure 23.2 An Ozobot Evo robot

Knowledge probe: Ozobot

Ozobot can be programmed using a free visual programming language called Blockly, which is converted to Javascript.

1   The following code (Figure 23.3) moves the robot in a square. Trace its logic carefully.

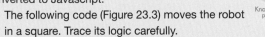

Figure 23.3

2   Draw a flowchart for this code.
3   Write structured English for this code.
4   Figure 23.4 shows the JavaScript for this code. JavaScript uses curly braces instead of indentation for the codes logical blocks. Can you understand it? count ++ adds one to count each time. It is equivalent to count = count + 1.

```
for (var count = 0; count < 4; count++) {
  move(FORWARD, 4, SPEED_MEDIUM);
  rotate(-90, SPEED_MEDIUM);
}
```

Figure 23.4

5   Follow the weblink from the *Digital Technologies 7 & 8* website for the Shapetracer tutorial and work through the 10 steps.
6   If you haven't done so before, see if you can get to level 10 in the Blockly Maze game.
7   If you are lucky enough to have access to an Ozobot, use the OzoBlockly Blockly editor and pick one of the levels 1–5. Tackle a challenge using the right hand panel (click 'brain' icon) (Figure 23.5).

Figure 23.5 Challenges provided in OzoBlockly

Taking it further

Try some of the other games at Blockly Games.

In *Digital Technologies 9 & 10* we will use Ozobot to learn a programming technique called recursion.

Lego EV3

There have been three generations of Lego programmable bricks and each can be used to program a robot. These are the yellow RCX brick, the NXT brick and the EV3 brick. Any of these are suitable for the robotics activities and projects outlined in this book.

LEGO® is a trademark of the LEGO Group of companies which does not sponsor, authorize or endorse this publication.

Figure 23.6 A basic EV3 model with two colour sensors

Robots have sensors, such as light sensors, that collect data and **actuators**, such as motors or speakers, to allow them to respond.

INTRODUCTORY PROJECT: ROBOTS DOING WHAT THEY'RE TOLD!

The task

Form a group of 2–3. Your task is to build a robotic vehicle that moves in paths that are common geometric shapes.

Defining

1 In this task, you are going to build a robot that moves in each of three geometric shapes: rectangle, isosceles triangle and hexagon.
2 Create the rectangle shape on the floor using masking tape.

Designing

1 Sketch a suitable design for the robot, identifying the wheels, axles, motors and sensor. If you wish, use one of the many standard designs for a basic robot available online. You could add a felt pen to draw the shapes as your robot moves.
2 Choose components from the LEGO or other kit to build the robot. Hint: the vehicle will need two motors to perform turns.
3 Build your robot. You may need to refer to resource material in your kit to help you.

Implementing

1 Program your robot to trace out a rectangle.
2 Load and run your program and observe results. Correct errors.
3 Turn your code into a single module for possible re-use or sharing. This is known as a *My Block* in Mindstorms.

Evaluating

1 Did your program run as expected? If not, make changes and run again.
2 Modify your program so your robot follows the same path but in the opposite direction.
3 Repeat this design cycle for isosceles triangle and hexagon.

Figure 23.7 In RoboCup, teams of autonomous robots play soccer against each other.

INFOBIT

One of the aims of the RoboCup contest is to build bipedal robots that can beat the FIFA World Champions by 2050! Follow the weblink from the *Digital Technologies 7 & 8* website to see it in action.

Weblink

EXTENSION: PROGRAM YOUR OWN AIRSHOW!

You will need:
• the free Tynker iOS or Android app
• a Sphero or supported Parrot drone.

The task

Your task is to use the free Tynker app, or equivalent, to control a small drone or Sphero.

If you have access to Android or iOS tablets, you can use the free Tynker app to control a drone or a Sphero (Figure 23.8).

Your drone will create your own airshow! IMPORTANT: Make sure people are not anywhere near your drone when flying it, and make sure you know where the button is to drop it to the ground in an emergency.

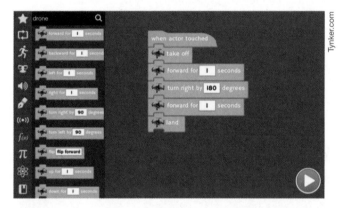

Figure 23.8

There are several types of Parrot-branded drones and mini drones available. A Parrot drone is one of many robotic devices that can be programmed with the free Tynker Blockly-based visual programming language via an iPad or iPhone. Code is uploaded via Bluetooth to the connected drone or a Sphero.

Apple's Swift programming language can also be used to program devices, including EV3 robots, drones and Spheros.

Figure 23.9

24

PROJECT: ROBO OLYMPICS

THE TASK

Your task is to design, build and program a robot to compete in three separate robotic Olympic events.

A robot may progress to the next event only after completing each event to the satisfaction of the team who designed it, and your teacher, who will sign off after each one.

Events may be completed in any order, but it is a competition. Points will be awarded for the best results.

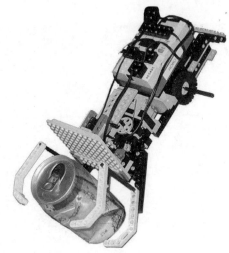

Figure 24.3 Mechanism for Robo Olympic can-grabber event

Robo Olympic rules

- Design, build, modify and program your robot to achieve the best possible result.
- You may have a trial run in each event before being judged.
- Your robot may be redesigned and reprogrammed before each event.
- You may use Internet research to help you build or program your robot; however, your teacher will award extra credit for original ideas.
- Your robot may have a maximum of three attempts for each event and the best of these will be your score.
- Document progress throughout the project using a spreadsheet.
- Judges will award points out of 10 for each result – the best overall team score wins the Robo Olympics!
- Judges participate in events but are scored in their own event by the teacher.

Figure 24.1 A Robo Olympic ramp-climbing event

Figure 24.2 A Robo Olympic line-following event

9780170411813

Defining

1 Form a group of students (2–3) and devise an event.
2 Your group establishes rules and scoring for their own event.
   Below are suggested Robo Olympic events for the robots to compete in:
   - Reach the top of an inclined slope. The steeper the slope, the more points.
   - A race against other robots.
   - Two robots playing tug-o-war, or two robots pushing each other out of a circle (as in sumo wrestling).
   - Follow a large, flat surface with a curved line.
   - Continually move within an open rectangle for one minute without becoming stranded.
   - Follow and escape a maze.
   - Recognise different coloured shapes.
   - Sense and lift an object.
   - Move a ball into a goal.
   - Push cans out of a circle, but not to leave the circle.
3 Each group describes their own event to the class, explaining how it will be judged and scored. Your teacher selects a few of the events, to suit the time available, and fine-tunes the marking schemes. Chosen events are announced. Rules and scoring are placed beside each event.
4 Decide roles (designers, builders, programmers, journal writers, testers).
5 Decide the order in which your group will tackle each event.
6 Discuss possible solutions for each event. Prepare for the event by discussing the rules with those designing the event.

Designing

1 Build and program your group's robot for your first event.
2 Design and use a collaborative online tool such as Google Docs to prepare a report after each event.
3 Do a test run (not counted towards your final score).
4 Modify your robot and reprogram to achieve efficiency.

Implementing

1 Take each challenge in turn. Refine your designs and repeat to a maximum of three attempts, counting the best score. Redesign and reprogram your robot after each event. Update scores in your spreadsheet.
2 Ask your teacher for extra credit if you believe you have added original ideas.

Evaluating

1 Judges from each design group provide performance feedback to the class.
2 Your group uses a collaborative tool such as Google Docs to compile a report on performances in each event, what you would do differently and the scores achieved.
3 What did you learn from this project?

_____

_____

_____

_____

_____

_____

_____

_____

_____

_____

4 Identify some additional features you could include.

_____

_____

_____

_____

_____

_____

_____

_____

_____

_____

_____

_____

25

PROJECT: SCI-FI SIMULATION

Note: Completing this project requires knowledge of basic principles from Chapter 3, including selection and looping control structures.

Lego's Mindstorms EV3 robotic kit is suitable for this project; however, other suitable systems can be used.

Figure 25.1 An EV3 robotics kit in use

This project covers a wide range of the outcomes in this course: collaboration, project management, programming, embedded systems, prototyping, modelling, simulation, design and robotics.

THE TASK

The first part of this task is to design and build a robotic system to simulate the cycles of a washing machine, including two different user selected cycles.

Using the skills you have acquired, you will then design a prototype for a machine suitable as a prop in a sci-fi (science fiction) movie.

Defining

1   Carefully examine the operation of a washing machine. Below is a typical washing machine sequence:
    - fill cycle (water on)
    - soak cycle with half tumbles (water off) (repeats multiple times)
    - tumble wash cycle clockwise and anticlockwise reusing water
    - rinse cycle (water on) using fresh water clockwise and anticlockwise
    - spin dry low speed clockwise and anticlockwise
    - spin dry high speed.

Knowledge probe: Embedded systems

Motors, lights and sensors are controlled by a computer inside the EV3. This is why such a system is called an embedded system. The main chip that controls the EV3 is called a microprocessor or a microcontroller.

Appliances such as coffee machines, washing machines, TVs, cameras, smartphones and microwave ovens all use embedded systems.

There are also many microcontrolled embedded systems in a modern car, including in the engine control system and the braking system. Autonomous vehicles now being developed will depend on embedded systems.

While you learn about robots, you are also learning a lot about embedded systems. You will learn more about embedded systems in *Digital Technologies 9 & 10*.

Knowledge Probe

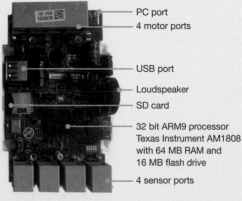

- PC port
- 4 motor ports
- USB port
- Loudspeaker
- SD card
- 32 bit ARM9 processor Texas Instrument AM1808 with 64 MB RAM and 16 MB flash drive
- 4 sensor ports

Figure 25.2 An embedded system: inside an EV3, showing ARM9 microprocessor chip

2   Search online to find an industrial Lego washing machine video.

3   Discuss and document what your project model will do.

_____

_____

_____

_____

Planning

1   Examine a real washing machine, set up an achievable goal, then design and build your simulation using your robotic hardware and software.

2   Describe two different wash sequences.

3   Assign team members to roles. The team should be aware of what others are working on:
    - building the model components
    - programming the model components
    - documenting the progress of the project (in a written format as well as taking pictures
    - drawing diagrams and other relevant documentation
    - Planning a timeframe for completing all parts of the project
    - selecting necessary parts.

    Your design should include:
    - the ability to select from two wash sequences using a switch
    - timing for cycles
    - a motor to imitate tub rotation
    - water heating, water entry and emptying indicated by labelled coloured LED lights.

Designing

1   Draw a flowchart.

2   Draw a diagram of your hardware design. Consider using Bricksmith (Mac) or Lego Digital designer (Win or Mac).

Producing

1   Construct your model.

2   Code, load and run your program.

Evaluating

1   Test the model with programs.

2   Have class members test your model.

3   Make modifications.

4   Did the model do what you planned?

5   Team members to complete documentation.

6   Demonstrate your project to the class.

Now, create your own sci-fi movie prop!

Now that you have experienced the design process by building this first machine, let your ideas go crazy!

Your group is to design a prototype of an interactive special effects prop to be used in a sci-fi movie – no limits! It must allow a user to select from a range of functions and have actuators (such as motors), which move in programmed ways.

You will be judged on design, creativity and technical ability. Start by searching images on the web of examples of sci-fi movie props.

Figure 25.3 Prototypes of props for a sci-fi movie

1   What did you learn from completing this project?

_____

_____

_____

Further ideas

- Create a vending machine. Follow the weblink from the *Digital Technologies 7 & 8* website to view a pictorial step-by-step guide. You could also Google 'Lego NXT vending machine' to view a video.
- Create a simulation of electronic equipment, such as a HD recorder with timed recording functions, using lights to simulate functions.

26

PROJECT: ROBOTS WALKING THE LINE

THE TASK

Your task is to develop your skills by successfully building a robot, then implement a standard one sensor line following program. After this task, you are to develop improved versions. The examples in this chapter use the Lego Mindstorms EV3 environment, but the principles apply to other systems.

Resources: You are to build your own robot with a limit of one colour/light sensor, your robot's programming software, two motors and two wheels. You will require a large surface with a continuous 20 mm wide black line, including a long straight section and curves of varying radii.

We suggest a design similar to Figure 26.1, using squares of cardboard or non-marking black tape on the floor.

1 Prepare your track.

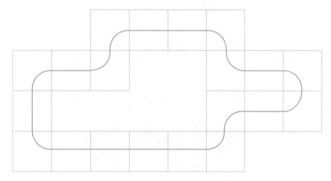

Figure 26.1 Suggested line following test track

2 Build your robot.

The basic robot design must have one sensor, two motors and two wheels. The recommendation is to include a pivot at the back.

You will need to test the best height above the ground for your sensor. Start at around 10 mm.

The arrangement of the sensor in relation to the robot's wheels and axis is very important. These form an isosceles triangle, with the sensor at the apex (Figure 26.2).

If the sensor is positioned too far from the axis it will turn in a wide arc and may miss tight curves. If the sensor is nearer the axis it can turn in a tighter arc.

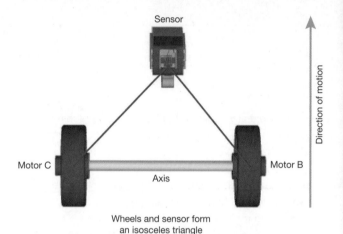

Figure 26.2 Viewed from above the robot, sensor and wheels form an isosceles triangle

Figure 26.3 Front and rear view of a successful line following robot (with front-wheel drive) with its sensor positioned between the wheels and close to the axis

9780170411813

Defining

Basic line follower using single sensor and motor blocks

Humans follow lines by seeing the 'big picture'. We can see the direction ahead and which side of a line we are on. A light sensor receives only a single item of data – the amount of light reaching it. It does not know on which side of the line it has strayed. If it is programmed to turn in a set direction when straying from a line (because the sensor 'sees' the reflected light increase) it may turn the wrong way.

A solution is to program a robot to follow the edge of a line by zigzagging along it.

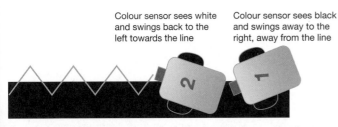

Colour sensor sees white and swings back to the left towards the line

Colour sensor sees black and swings away to the right, away from the line

Figure 26.4 Using one sensor, a robot can follow a line by following its edge.

Most sensors can make continuous readings from 100 (pure white) to 0 (pure black).

A two-wheeled robot can be made to turn by shutting off one motor. Suppose the robot is on the right edge of the line, moving from right to left (see Figure 26.4). Using only

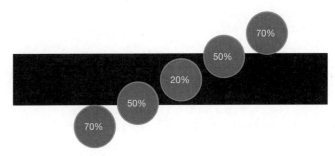

Figure 26.5 A colour sensor measures different reflected light intensities as its position varies over a black line.

one sensor, you can make the robot swing right (away from a line) when the sensor is over the black line, and thus reads a low-light reading. Its reading drops below halfway (called the 'threshold value'). It then swings left towards the line when it shows a value above the threshold. Following is the algorithm written using structured English:

```
WHILE True
   IF sensor < threshold light value
   THEN
      Motor B OFF
      Motor C ON
   ELSE
      Motor B ON
      Motor C OFF
   ENDIF
ENDWHILE
```

Figure 26.6 shows a block diagram program using Mindstorms EV3 software with motor blocks.

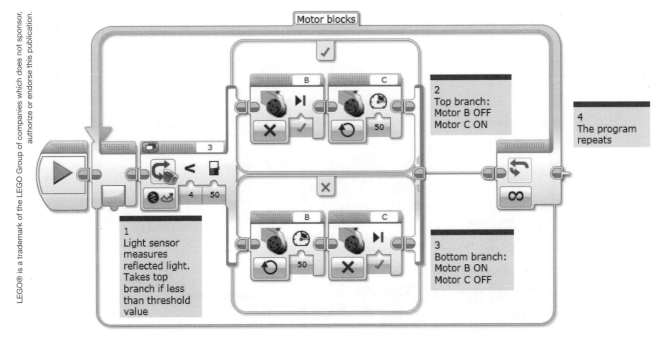

Motor blocks

1
Light sensor measures reflected light. Takes top branch if less than threshold value

2
Top branch:
Motor B OFF
Motor C ON

3
Bottom branch:
Motor B ON
Motor C OFF

4
The program repeats

Figure 26.6 A basic line edge follower program using motor blocks showing a threshold of 50

Line follower using motor blocks

1   Find out how to measure light levels manually using your sensor. Room lighting can have a big effect on your threshold value. Measure the light level for pure white and for pure black. Set a value halfway between these:
Threshold = (white level – black level) ÷ 2

2   Build your code using motor blocks, using Figure 26.6 as your guide, and adjust the threshold value to suit.

3   Test the algorithm using your robot.

4   On which side of the line must the robot be placed for this algorithm to work?

5   Comment on the result.

6   The code is not reliable if the robot is negotiating tight curves. Explain why.

Basic line follower using single sensor and steering block

Instead of controlling the motors, you could use a *steering block* (if available in your software) to control both motors at once. Below is a much simpler algorithm written using structured English:

```
WHILE True
  IF sensor < threshold light value
  THEN
    steer right
  ELSE
    steer left
  ENDIF
ENDWHILE
```

Figure 26.7 shows a block diagram program using Mindstorms EV3 software with steering blocks.

Within the loop are two branches. Suppose the robot is placed as shown in Figure 26.4. When the light is below the set threshold value, the top branch is selected: motor B slows and our robot turns right.

If the light is more than our threshold, the bottom branch is selected: motor C slows and the robot turns left.

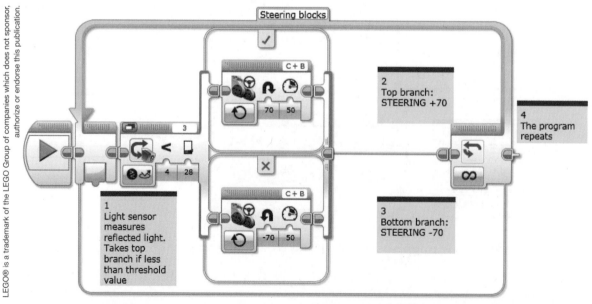

LEGO® is a trademark of the LEGO Group of companies which does not sponsor, authorize or endorse this publication.

Steering blocks

C + B

70   50

2
Top branch:
STEERING +70

4
The program repeats

3

<

4   28

1
Light sensor measures reflected light. Takes top branch if less than threshold value

C + B

-70   50

3
Bottom branch:
STEERING -70

Figure 26.7 A basic line follower using steering blocks showing threshold set at 28

9780170411813

Line follower using single sensor and steering block

1   Use your robot's software to implement this basic line follower using a single sensor with a steering block instead of controlling the motors directly. Build your code using steering blocks, using Figure 26.7 as your guide, and adjust the threshold value to suit.

Skill builder

2   Explain why this code causes a robot to 'follow' a black line and explain where the robot must be placed for it to work.

_____

_____

_____

_____

_____

_____

_____

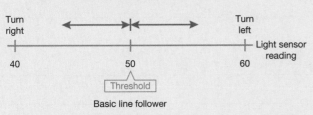

Basic line follower

Figure 26.8 Robot turns left when light reduces and right when light increases

Designing

Improving the design 1

Is your robot better at keeping to a straight line? Is your robot better at managing the curves? Can you reduce zigzagging further?

Instead of setting a single threshold, you could set a middle range where the robot does not turn at all.

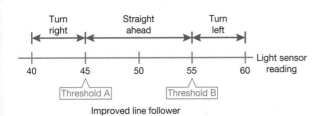

Improved line follower

Figure 26.9 Robot does not turn when values lie between A and B

1   Use this idea to redesign your algorithm.
2   Test this design using your robot. Comment on the result.

_____

_____

_____

_____

_____

Improving the design 2

Light measure from the sensor changes smoothly from its maximum (when over white) to its minimum (when over black). Instead of switching your motors suddenly to lower power to turn your robot, why not control steering directly using this smoothly varying difference between the sensor's light measure and your threshold?

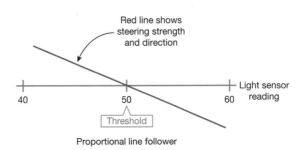

Proportional line follower

Figure 26.10 Power to steering is controlled directly using the difference between threshold and measured light

To do this, you need to learn how to use constants and variables in your code. Use this idea to redesign your algorithm.

Below is this approach written in structured English:

```
WHILE True
    set threshold value 'a'
    measure light intensity 'b'
    calculate 'a - b'
    multiply by some constant value to
      make this a larger value e.g.
      20*(a-b)
    adjust steering by this value
ENDWHILE
```

There are many ways to implement this algorithm. Figure 26.11 shows one approach (using Mindstorms EV3 software). Figure 26.12 shows the same algorithm using this software's advanced maths block.

Implementing

1 Build and fine-tune the best version of your line follower.
2 Test this design using your robot. Comment on the result.

_____

_____

_____

_____

_____

Evaluating

1 Test and further improve your version. Consider:
  • different heights of sensor above the surface
  • changing position of sensor

• changing position of wheels in relation to sensor
• exchanging ideas with other groups
• creating code connected to a touch sensor to more easily calibrate light levels.

Web probe: Advanced algorithms

In *Digital Technologies 9 & 10* you will study a more complicated control approach called PID. Research 'PID line follower' online and see if you can summarise the way it works.

_____

_____

_____

_____

_____

_____

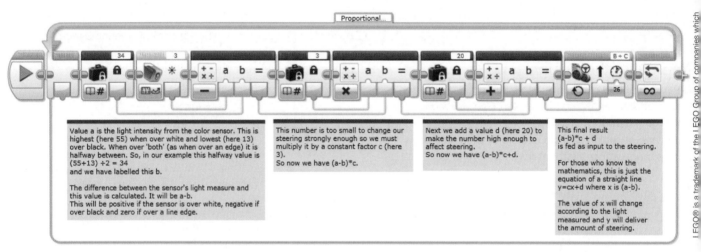

Value a is the light intensity from the color sensor. This is highest (here 55) when over white and lowest (here 13) over black. When over 'both' (as when over an edge) it is halfway between. So, in our example this halfway value is (55+13) ÷2 = 34
and we have labelled this b.

The difference between the sensor's light measure and this value is calculated. It will be a-b.
This will be positive if the sensor is over white, negative if over black and zero if over a line edge.

This number is too small to change our steering strongly enough so we must multiply it by a constant factor c (here 3).
So now we have (a-b)*c.

Next we add a value d (here 20) to make the number high enough to affect steering.
So now we have (a-b)*c+d.

This final result
(a-b)*c + d
is fed as input to the steering.

For those who know the mathematics, this is just the equation of a straight line y=cx+d where x is (a-b).

The value of x will change according to the light measured and y will deliver the amount of steering.

Figure 26.11 Example of a proportional line follower using three maths calculation blocks. The notes explain the way the variables are used.

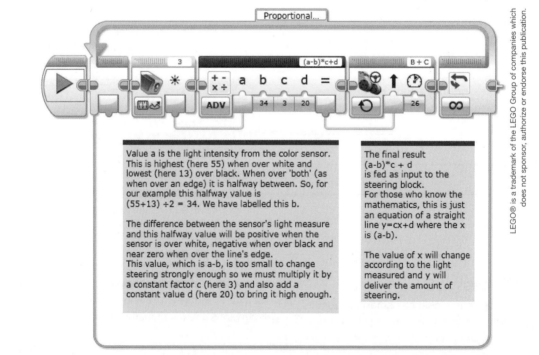

Value a is the light intensity from the color sensor. This is highest (here 55) when over white and lowest (here 13) over black. When over 'both' (as when over an edge) it is halfway between. So, for our example this halfway value is (55+13) ÷2 = 34. We have labelled this b.

The difference between the sensor's light measure and this halfway value will be positive when the sensor is over white, negative when over black and near zero when over the line's edge.
This value, which is a-b, is too small to change steering strongly enough so we must multiply it by a constant factor c (here 3) and also add a constant value d (here 20) to bring it high enough.

The final result
(a-b)*c + d
is fed as input to the steering block.
For those who know the mathematics, this is just an equation of a straight line y=cx+d where the x is (a-b).

The value of x will change according to the light measured and y will deliver the amount of steering.

Figure 26.12 A revised version of Figure 26.11, using one maths block to replace three. The notes explain the way the variables are used.